THE VACCINE

ANSWERBOOK™

200 Essential Answers to Help You Make the Right Decisions for Your Child

— JAMIE LOEHR, MD, FAAFP —

SOURCEBOOKS, INC.®
NAPERVILLE, ILLINOIS

Published by Sourcebooks, Inc.
P.O. Box 4410, Naperville, Illinois 60567-4410
(630) 961-3900
Fax: (630) 961-2168
www.sourcebooks.com

Library of Congress Cataloging-in-Publication Data

Loehr, Jamie.
  The vaccine answer book : 200 essential answers to help you make the right
decisions for your child / by Jamie Loehr.
      p. cm.
  1. Vaccination of children—Popular works. 2. Immunization of children—
Popular works. I. Title.
  RJ240.L64 2009
  614.4'7083—dc22
                                2009012845

Printed and bound in the United States of America.
VP 10 9 8 7 6 5 4 3 2 1

Contents

Part III: Other Childhood Vaccines

Dedication

For my wonderful family:
Devon, Kieran, Shannon, and Mariah.
And most of all, Caitlin.
J.L.

Acknowledgments

My thanks go to my editor Sara Appino, and to my agent Grace Freedson, both of whom were instrumental in the creation of this book. Thanks to Jen Meyers, the coauthor of my first two books, and also to Leslie Daniels for getting me started on the path to writing.

Thanks to my parents Joan and Ray Loehr and my seven brothers and sisters for their love, advice, and support over the years. Thanks also to all the parents and children I have known in and out of my practice who have helped shape my knowledge and experiences.

To my family goes my biggest, most heartfelt appreciation. Their limitless understanding, humor, and love during the writing of this book made it all possible. Thanks to Devon, Kieran, Shannon, and Mariah, but most of all to Caitlin. I love you!

Introduction

As a practicing family physician with a special interest in pediatrics, I regularly find myself answering questions about vaccines. Parents are nervous about vaccines. Many parents have heard horror stories about complications from vaccines and are wondering if they have to worry about their child developing autism or seizures or encephalitis. They are also worried about milder side effects like fevers, about the ingredients in vaccines, and about their children receiving multiple vaccines at once.

At the same time, most parents recognize the benefits of vaccines. Even if they have never personally seen a case of polio or meningitis, they understand the damage these illnesses used to cause in our country. They intuitively understand the danger that their child could be normal on one day and be in the hospital fighting for his life the next day. And so they want the protection these vaccines offer, as long as the protection doesn't come at too high a price.

Over the past eighteen years, I have spent count-less hours counseling families about vaccines, discussing the benefits and risks of each vaccine in detail as well as the personal and public health benefits of vaccines in general. Over time, I came to realize that most physicians don't have the time or inclination to cover this material in depth. So, when I was offered the opportunity to write a question and answer book on vaccines, I jumped at the chance to articulate on paper many of the conversations I have shared with families over time.

You will realize as you read this book that I am in favor of vaccines. If you don't have any reasons to not vaccinate your child, I will recommend all vaccines to you. In both my personal and professional life, I feel the benefits of vaccines outweigh the risks. Thus, I have given the recommended vaccines to my own four children and also offer them to my patients.

However, you will also come to understand that I feel that some vaccines are more important than others. While I recommend them all, if I have parents who are so hesitant about vaccines that they are considering not vaccinating at all, I will suggest an alternative schedule, delaying less important vaccines until their child is older.

How do I decide which vaccines are more important? There are several factors. First, we need to know how common an illness is in the community and how serious the disease is. A vaccine for a disease that is common and serious is more important than a vaccine for a disease that is rare with only mild symptoms. Second, how safe is the vaccine? What are the potential side effects, and how often do they happen? And if the side effect occurs, are there any long-term consequences? I go over a formal risk-benefit analysis for vaccines in chapter 5.

I have several core beliefs underlying my attitudes toward vaccines. In order for you to better understand my thinking, I will articulate those beliefs here:

I believe vaccines are effective at preventing disease.

In short, vaccines work. They do what they are designed to do, which is to protect the recipient from certain diseases. So if you receive a vaccine for chickenpox, you are less likely to develop chickenpox if you are ever exposed to the disease in the future. And if a whole community receives the vaccine, the number of cases of chickenpox will decline in that community.

The proof that vaccines work is all around us. There have been fewer cases of chickenpox in the United States ever since that particular vaccine became commonly used. And there are fewer cases of measles, mumps, and rubella, fewer cases of polio, tetanus, and diphtheria, in the United States than there were fifty years ago. To use just one specific example, there were millions of cases of measles in the United States every year before 1950. Between 2000 and 2007, there were fewer than one hundred cases per year.

Some people argue that vaccines are not responsible for this rapid decrease in certain illnesses. Instead, they cite improved nutrition and sanitation in the United States as the reason for improved health and the corresponding drop in infectious diseases. While this is certainly part of the equation for some illnesses, such as hepatitis A, it is not the only explanation, and it is rarely the major contributing factor.

For other illnesses, improved sanitation and nutrition are clearly irrelevant. In 1985 there were over twenty thousand cases of severe Haemophilus influenzae type B (HiB) meningitis in the United States. In 1995, there were only one hundred cases. The HiB vaccine came into widespread use in the late 1980s. No one can argue that the United States had better nutrition or sanitation from 1985 to 1995. The logical conclusion is that the disease was almost wiped out in the United States by the vaccine.

Chickenpox is another example. Why would improved sanitation and nutrition wipe out measles and mumps and rubella but not chickenpox? In the 1950s there were millions of cases of these diseases. In the 1980s there were still millions of cases of chickenpox but only hundreds or at most thousands of cases of measles and mumps and rubella. The difference is that vaccines for measles, mumps, and rubella came out in the 1950s and 1960s, but the chickenpox vaccine didn't come into widespread use until the 1990s.

This doesn't mean that vaccines are unequivocally wonderful. You might still argue that the side effects are too risky or that a given vaccine is not cost-effective or that a certain disease is so mild that we don't need a vaccine. But people who say vaccines don't work are simply wrong.

And in the end, you want them to be wrong; you want vaccines to work. Back in the 1950s, parents lived in fear of certain infectious diseases. They knew of a child who had been hospitalized with complications from measles; they knew someone paralyzed with polio or of a baby who had died of pertussis. They were desperate to protect their children from these illnesses.

Even today, you want vaccines to work. If you are going to be exposed to yellow fever in South

America, a disease with a 50 percent fatality rate if you happen to contract it, you are glad that a vaccine exists. You want to be sure the vaccine works as best as it possibly can.

I believe herd immunity is effective at preventing disease and that it is our responsibility as citizens of our community to do what we can to maintain herd immunity.

Herd immunity is the concept that you don't need 100 percent immunity in a population to wipe out a disease. Instead, if a certain threshold of people is immune to a certain disease, then even those who are not immune will have a much lower chance of catching the disease. This occurs because there are fewer and fewer people who can spread it in the community. For most diseases, the threshold is around 90 percent. In other words, once more than 90 percent of a population is immune, the disease becomes much rarer than you would expect based on vaccination rates alone. In some cases, like with smallpox, the disease might even be wiped out.

Herd immunity is helpful because it is impossible to achieve 100 percent immunity. Some individuals won't become immune even after being vaccinated. And some individuals should not receive a vaccine for medical reasons. So there will always be some

individuals in a population who are not immune to a given disease. However, if the community has passed the necessary threshold, the resulting herd immunity will still provide protection to nonimmune individuals from a given illness.

I believe nothing in life is guaranteed and that sometimes bad things happen without any explanation.

These two concepts are critical in understanding my attitude toward vaccinations. On the one hand, vaccines are not perfect. There is no guarantee that if you receive a vaccine, you will become immune. Some of the rates of protection are over 98 percent, but no one can ever guarantee 100 percent immunity. So it is still possible to contract a disease even after receiving a vaccine. The vaccine makes it less likely that you will get the disease and often leads to a milder illness if you do end up contracting the disease, but you can't assume 100 percent protection from any given vaccine.

On the other hand, the natural history of the diseases themselves is not guaranteed. Most people who get chickenpox have an annoying rash and fever for seven to ten days. However, some people end up in the hospital because of complications from the chickenpox. They might acquire pneumonia or a skin infection that requires antibiotics. In very rare circumstances, people die of complications from chickenpox. That is incredibly uncommon: there were only forty deaths a year in the United States in the prevaccination era, but still, they happened. Even as benign a disease as chickenpox can occasionally be life threatening. Nothing in life is guaranteed.

As for bad outcomes, they are often random and unpredictable. We know that, on average, one child in fourteen thousand will develop a seizure after receiving a DTaP vaccine, but we don't know which child that will be. You hope it will not be your child, but you don't know.

And while you do your best to protect your child from dangers, sometimes bad things still happen. I have some parents tell me that they don't want to vaccinate because they don't think their baby is at particular risk. They are breast-feeding and are not using any kind of day care. While it is very true that breast-feeding and avoiding day care lowers that baby's risk of contracting many dangerous diseases, it doesn't lower the risk to zero. There are still plenty of chances for exposure to certain diseases, from a random exposure to a friend in the grocery store to a relative who might share the disease while visiting to an unknown source in the community. And the protection a baby receives from his or her mother's breast milk is nowhere near the protection received from a vaccine.

A dramatic example of both of these concepts occurs when meningococcal meningitis strikes a college student. Here we have a healthy young adult, walking around campus with no medical concerns at all, and twenty-four hours later she is in the ICU fighting for her life. The scary thought is that many people carry the bacteria around in their upper respiratory tract without ever knowing they are carriers or even becoming slightly ill. So why does one particular person develop this life-threatening disease? We don't know. Bad things beyond our control still sometimes happen.

I believe that the risks of vaccines and the risk of various diseases need to be thought of in terms of statistics. However, most people have a hard time understanding complex statistics, especially those involving very small numbers.

Some vaccines protect against very common diseases. Before the 1950s, there were millions of cases of measles and mumps and chickenpox every year. These were common diseases that swept through a community and parents expected their children to get sick sooner or later. So when vaccines against these diseases were created, we were able to prevent millions of episodes of illness with just one vaccine. That shows a very good return on our investment.

However, sometimes the disease in question is rarer. Haemophilus influenzae type B (HiB) can lead to a devastating illness in children, including meningitis, an infection of the fluid surrounding the brain and spinal cord, and sepsis, a bloodstream infection. The HiB vaccine mentioned earlier is one of the best vaccines we have today. It is very effective with only minimal side effects. Before the vaccine was developed, there were about twenty thousand cases of these dangerous HiB infections in the United States every year. In 2007, there were fewer than one hundred cases.

However, there are approximately four million babies born in the United States every year. If you assume all twenty thousand cases of invasive HiB disease that existed in the prevaccine era occurred in the first year of life (which is not completely accurate), you will see that we are vaccinating four million babies every year to prevent twenty thousand severe illnesses.

In other words, you have to vaccinate two hundred babies to prevent one case of HiB meningitis. In fact, because babies usually receive three doses of the HiB vaccine in the first year of life, you have to give six hundred shots to prevent one case of HiB meningitis. And that is the most cost-effective vaccine we use.

What happens when the illness itself becomes rare because of the mass vaccination campaign? Instead of four million cases of measles, we now usually have fewer than one hundred cases every year in the United States. These rare events are where the game of statistics becomes harder to comprehend. If the disease is rare and the side effects of the vaccine are rare, how should we decide what to do? In this situation, some parents wonder if the risk of side effects from a given vaccine is greater than the risk of getting the disease.

The average human brain has a hard time comprehending these kinds of statistics. When it comes to personal decisions, we might understand a one in two risk (fifty/fifty) or maybe even a one in ten or one in one hundred risk. However, when we get to a one in one thousand or one in ten thousand or one in one million risk, it is harder to comprehend what those numbers mean when it comes to our own personal risk. We usually just lump them into the category of "rare."

However, there is a big difference between one in one thousand and one in one million. If there are three hundred million people in the United States, a one in one million risk of contracting an infection would mean that three hundred people would develop the disease. However, a one in one thousand risk would mean that three hundred thousand people would develop the disease, a significant difference.

Many of the side effects of vaccines and many of the rare consequences of a given illness occur at a rate of one in one thousand to one in one million. If we actually do the math, we might rationally be able to say that a one in one thousand risk of brain damage from a disease is greater than a one in one million risk of brain damage from a disease. However, if we are simply lumping both risks together as "rare," we don't comprehend that one risk is actually a thousand times greater than the other.

Furthermore, our emotions come into play when comparing the tiny risks of a vaccine and the tiny risks of a disease. Some of my patients feel that they would rather take the risk of a natural process, like a disease, instead of an artificial process, like a vaccine. They also tell me they would feel less guilty if their child had a bad outcome from the natural process instead of one where they actively intervened to give their child the vaccine. Even if the numerical risks are the same, emotionally we may view them very differently.

I have a general but not complete trust in the medical establishment.

I bring this up because I have a number of families in my practice who choose not to vaccinate because they don't trust the medical establishment. They may not trust the researchers who do the studies, the corporations that produce the vaccines, and/or the government organizations that make the recommendations for or against vaccines.

In response, I have to acknowledge the imperfections of the current medical environment. I recognize that conflicts of interest exist and that research is sometimes funded by pharmaceutical corporations. I understand that these corporations want to sell more vaccines in order to make money. I see that many organizations seem to favor public health issues over those of individual families.

And I know that the medical establishment is sometimes wrong. I have been practicing long enough to see some of these mistakes, to see what was once gospel truth repudiated, replaced by a diametrically opposite opinion. An example of a literal 180-degree shift is the recommendation to have babies sleep on their backs. For years doctors told parents to let their young babies sleep on their tummies in order to protect them from reflux and aspiration. However, experts now believe that sleeping on the back is safer because studies show it decreases the risk of Sudden Infant Death Syndrome (SIDS) by 50 percent. Physicians now strongly encourage parents to put babies on their backs to sleep.

So medicine is not perfect. But I still believe in the process. I still believe in using good science and good-quality, unbiased studies to guide decisions. Maybe not one study or two studies, but if many independent studies point in the same direction, it suggests the truth is in that direction. Furthermore, I believe that most people are trying to do a good job, that they want to make effective vaccines, and that they don't want to make mistakes.

And I believe in the public health organizations that make the vaccine recommendations. They are trying to protect children and keep them healthy. As I discuss in chapter 9, in the late 1990s the Centers for Disease Control and Prevention (CDC) recommended that a certain rotavirus vaccine be pulled from the market because it had an increased risk of a certain kind of bowel obstruction. The absolute increase in risk was low, but it was enough to recommend against the vaccine. This action reassured me that the CDC was not simply an automatic rubber stamp in favor of all vaccines.

I believe that parents have the right to make medical decisions for their children and that adults have the right to make medical decisions for themselves.

With very few exceptions, the locus of medical decision making in the United States is in the individual or, in the case of a child, in the parents. Individuals and parents decide whether or not they want X rays or blood tests or whether to take medicine for their infection or their asthma. They even get to decide if they want to allow a doctor to examine them in the first place! The theory behind this concept of autonomy is that individuals and parents have absolute control over the integrity of their bodies and their children's bodies, and nothing may be done without appropriate permission.

However, as I discuss in chapter 4, vaccines fall within the category of public health. While no one can force parents to vaccinate their children, all states have laws requiring certain vaccinations in order to attend day care or public schools. In addition, there is also a law that children must receive an education. In some cases, parents clearly feel forced to vaccinate their children because they are unable to homeschool them.

This leads to an interesting dilemma between individual autonomy and the interests of public health.

Although there are exemptions to these vaccination laws, in the majority of states the requirements for exemptions are hard to meet. In the end, though, parents (almost) always have the final say on whether or not their child receives a vaccination.

I believe that my job as a physician is to give my patients all the information they need to make a decision, but it is their job to make the final decision.

The era of "doctor knows best" has been over for many years. In its place we have a partnership between me as the doctor and you and your family as the patients. My goal is to give you enough information so that you can make the best decision for yourself and your family.

Implicit in this belief is that there is not one "right" decision. You and I might disagree about the best choice in a given situation. However, as long as you have the necessary facts and understand the implications of your decision, then your decision is the "right" one for you.

Part of this decision-making process is sharing information both ways. Not only do I want to tell you what I think are the most important aspects of the decision, but I also want to hear your thinking as you process the decision. You might have a perspective I have never encountered before. Or you might have incorrect information that I can try to correct. In the end, though, the final decision is yours.

The rest of this book is my effort to give you the information you need to understand the different vaccinations that are available in the United States today. Then you, with the help of your own physicians, can make the best decisions regarding vaccines for yourself and your family. I hope you find this information useful. I've enjoyed sharing my thoughts with you.

Part I
Understanding Vaccines

Chapter 1

VACCINE BASICS

- What is a vaccine?
- What are bacteria?
- What is a virus?
- What is a microorganism? What is a pathogen?
- What is an infection? What is an illness?
- How does your body's immune system normally fight off an infection?
- How does a vaccine work?
- What is an immune globulin injection?
- What are the different kinds of vaccines and how are they made?
- How effective are vaccines?
- How are vaccines given?
- What is a Vaccine Information Statement?
- What are some common side effects of vaccines?
- How can I prevent or manage minor side effects from vaccines?
- How do you dose pain medication for children?
- What are some rare and/or more severe side effects of vaccines?

What is a vaccine?

A vaccine is a substance or a preparation that is introduced into your body in order to stimulate an immune response against a specific viral or bacterial microorganism. After that immune response has matured, if you are ever exposed to that microorganism again, you should be protected from the infection and either not get the disease or at most get a mild case. Vaccines enable your body to become immune to a disease without ever having the illness.

What are bacteria?

Bacteria are single-celled microorganisms that contain all the basic building blocks of a cell, such as DNA, RNA, cell walls, and cell organelles. The word *bacterium* is the singular form for the plural form *bacteria*. Bacteria reproduce by dividing their DNA and RNA into two parts and then building up cell walls to divide the one cell into two cells.

Bacteria are all around us. They are everywhere: on your skin, in your nose, in your intestines, and on every object that you touch or eat. But don't worry. Most bacteria in the world are either helpful from the perspective of humans (such as bacteria that break down waste products) or at least not harmful. Bacteria that are harmful to humans are relatively rare. About

40 percent of the vaccines available in the United States are targeted against harmful bacteria.

What is a virus?

A virus is a collection of nucleic acid, either DNA or RNA, surrounded by a protein coat, which replicates within the cell of another organism. Viruses are interesting in that they have no cell of their own and rely on the host cell's machinery to replicate their nucleic acid. Viruses also use the host cell's machinery to create capsids, the protein shells that surround and protect the viral nucleic acid.

The life cycle of a virus consists of attaching the virus capsid to a cell membrane of the host cell and then inserting the viral DNA or RNA into the cell. After the host cell has copied the viral nucleic acid and manufactured the virus, the host cell is destroyed. This action releases thousands of capsids and allows new viruses to spread to other cells. The majority of vaccines available in the United States are targeted against harmful viruses.

What is a microorganism? What is a pathogen?

A microorganism is a living entity that is so small it can only be seen with the aid of a microscope.

A pathogen is an organism that causes disease. Examples of pathogens include bacteria, viruses, parasites, and fungi. Note that a pathogen does not have to be a microorganism; some parasitic worms cause disease and are pathogens but are large enough to be seen with the naked eye. In addition, a microorganism is not necessarily a pathogen. Bacteria can only be seen with a microscope, but most bacteria do not cause disease. All vaccines are targeted against pathogenic bacteria or viruses. We do not (yet) have any vaccines against fungi or parasites.

What is an infection? What is an illness?

An infection can be defined as the presence of a pathogen in your body. When the pathogen invades your body and replicates, it occasionally leads to certain kinds of damage. This damage occurs either because the pathogen directly attacks the cells in your body or because your body's immune system creates collateral damage when it fights off the pathogen. An *illness*, or the sensation of feeling sick, is a result of this damage.

Note that sometimes the illness is not caused by the pathogen but rather by the body's response to the pathogen. At times the body overreacts, and the extreme inflammatory response to the pathogen is what causes the most harm.

Also note that an infection does not necessarily

have to lead to an illness. There are times when the body keeps the infection under control with no damage to the body. An example would be people who are carriers for *N. meningitides*, the bacteria that can lead to meningitis. Some individuals carry the bacteria around in their noses and respiratory tracts without ever becoming sick.

How does your body's immune system normally fight off an infection?

Your body contains certain blood cells, called white blood cells (WBCs), which fight infections. One subset of these WBCs is called lymphocytes, which can be divided into two main teams: T cells *and* B cells. The T cells and B cells can be further subdivided into categories, such as helper T cells or memory B cells.

In addition, your body has another subset of white blood cells called phagocytes, which specialize in search-and-destroy missions. These phagocytes find and then "eat" foreign particles such as bacteria, viruses, and fungi. They also clean up after dead or injured cells.

When your body is exposed to a new pathogen, say the chickenpox virus, the phagocytes are the first line of defense. Some of the phagocytes, called granulocytes, continue to eat as much virus as they can until they die. Other phagocytes, the macrophages and dendritic cells, also ingest the virus, but their goal is to take a chickenpox virus protein back to the immune system to raise the alarm. They travel to the nearest lymph node and present this viral protein to lots and lots of B cells and helper T cells. These phagocytes are looking for particular cells that contain the appropriate receptor that matches the chickenpox virus protein. When they find the match, it activates that special helper T cell, which then initiates the rest of the immune cascade.

But how is it possible for your body to have a certain helper T cell to match any given protein from all the possible microorganisms in the world? To oversimplify a complicated process, the body is able to create different receptors by combining the basic receptor building blocks in various patterns. Imagine having dozens of different size and different color Lego blocks. If you were fast enough and had enough hands, you could create millions of different shapes out of those blocks. If you had enough patterns, then you could likely find a match for the shape and color of any foreign block that wandered into your neighborhood.

It seems unbelievable, but the immune system has found a way to create millions of helper T cell receptors so that it can match practically any foreign microorganism that wanders into the body. The immune system does the same thing for B cells, which will become important in a few moments. This flexibility is the beauty of the immune system.

Now back to the fight against the chickenpox virus. When the helper T cell is activated, it makes multiple copies of itself, including some specialized cells called memory T cells. The helper T cells also produce activating proteins that are able to activate killer T cells. The killer T cells begin to patrol the body, searching for any cells infected by the virus. The infected cells are marked because when the virus entered a given cell, it left a protein on the outside of the cell wall. If the killer T cell sees that protein, it destroys the cell before it can release any more viruses.

If you go back a few steps, you will notice that the phagocytes presented the chickenpox virus protein to both helper T cells *and* B cells. When the virus protein matches a particular B cell, it partially activates that B cell. However, if the activating T cell protein comes into contact with a partially activated B cell, the B cell becomes fully activated. The activated B cell then starts to divide into two sets of cells: plasma cells and memory B cells.

Plasma cells are specialized to produce antibodies, which are small proteins that match the receptor on the surface of the original B cell. Remember that the chickenpox virus protein matched the receptor on the B cell that turned into this particular plasma cell. This means that the antibodies produced by the plasma cell will also match the chickenpox virus protein. Plasma cells can produce thousands of antibodies per second. These antibodies swarm all over the body and attach themselves to any chickenpox virus they find.

When the virus is coated with antibodies, it becomes an easy target for the phagocytic cells. These cells either eat and destroy the virus or present the chickenpox virus protein to the B cells and helper T cells, starting the whole cycle over again.

So what about the memory B cells and the memory T cells? These cells are programmed to have a prolonged life. Their presence allows the body to react more quickly to a repeat exposure to the chickenpox virus.

The first time your body sees the chickenpox virus, it takes over two weeks to create all the necessary antibodies to fight off the infection. However, if you have already had the infection, the memory B and T cells already exist in your body, and you are able to mass produce antibodies much more quickly. Within just a few days, there are billions of antibodies available to attack the virus, and you don't get sick. This is why it is rare to ever get chickenpox twice.

But even though it is rare to get chickenpox twice, it is not impossible. About 1 percent of people diagnosed with chickenpox will get the disease a second time. This occurs because it is possible for your immunity to wane. It might be that your body didn't make many of the memory cells in the first place. Or it might be that you lost those memory cells over time. Whatever the reason, this just goes to show that the body is not perfect.

How does a vaccine work?

As previously described in detail, a pathogen stimulates your immune system to create antibodies and memory cells that fight against a given disease. A vaccine harnesses the same process but allows the body to create the antibodies and memory cells *without having to suffer through the complete illness*! The key step is that instead of using the actual pathogen as the stimulating agent, the vaccine presents either a weakened or attenuated form of the pathogen, or inactive parts of the pathogen.

These slightly different stimulating agents are still sufficient for your immune system to create the necessary, long-living memory cells. These memory cells will help your body fight off the original pathogen if you are ever exposed to the disease in the future. In other words, you become immune to the pathogen.

However, these slightly different agents are not able to give you the complete illness. Instead, you will either have no symptoms or at most develop a milder form of the disease.

What is an immune globulin injection?

An immune globulin injection is the administration of antibodies that provide protection against certain diseases. Unlike a vaccine, which stimulates the body to produce its own antibodies, an immune globulin injection provides prefabricated antibodies that have been filtered from other people's bodies. An immune globulin injection is useful if you don't have the two or three weeks of time needed to wait for a vaccine to become effective. For example, if you are suddenly traveling overseas to a country where you might be exposed to the hepatitis A virus, you need protection immediately and don't have time to wait for the vaccine to work.

The major drawback to an immune globulin injection is that the protection will fade as the antibodies are slowly destroyed over three to four months. For this reason, an immune globulin injection is often given at the same time as a vaccine. A common example is giving both the rabies immune globulin injection and the rabies vaccine when someone is exposed to a rabid animal. The antibodies in the immune globulin injection will work immediately to protect the recipient from the disease, while the vaccine will stimulate the long-term production of the body's own antibodies.

What are the different kinds of vaccines and how are they made?

There are several methods of making vaccines. One method uses an inactivated, or killed, organism as the immune system stimulant. The body is exposed to the entire microorganism, but since it has been killed, it cannot make you sick. An example of this type of vaccine is the injectable polio vaccine.

Another method uses a weakened, or attenuated, virus as the stimulant. In this case, the organism has been carefully weakened but not killed. Again, the body sees the entire organism and develops a full immune response to the vaccine. However, the weakened virus can only give you at most a mild version of the disease. Examples of this type of vaccine include measles, mumps, rubella, and chickenpox vaccines as well as the oral polio vaccine.

A third method of making vaccines involves using certain sugars or proteins from the pathogen as the immune system stimulant. This is done in two ways. In some cases, the sugars are linked to another protein in order to boost the immune response. This process is called polysaccharide conjugation. In another process, genetic engineering is used to produce specified proteins that act as the immune system stimulant. These special proteins are called recombinant vaccines. With both these types of vaccines, only parts of the pathogen are present, so it is impossible to get the disease from the vaccine. Examples of these methods include HiB, which is a polysaccharide conjugate vaccine, and hepatitis B, which is a recombinant vaccine.

How effective are vaccines?

Vaccines are extremely effective, although some are better at preventing diseases than others. If you simply measure the body's ability to produce antibodies to fight a specific disease, vaccines are very effective, with an over 95 percent success rate for many of the common vaccines. Real-world protection is usually higher because of herd immunity (see page 29 in chapter 2).

This does not mean that vaccines are perfect. Nothing protects 100 percent of the people 100 percent of the time. To use a specific example, only 98 percent of people who receive the normal three-dose series of the hepatitis B vaccine develop antibodies. Some people can get up to nine vaccinations of hepatitis B without any response! In the case of hepatitis B, it appears that a slight genetic abnormality in the immune system prevents the vaccine from working in some individuals.

In addition, as previously mentioned, immunity can fade over time. One example of this involves the chickenpox vaccine. Recent studies have shown that about 15 percent of children who received the vaccine at twelve to fifteen months still were able to contract the illness four to five years later. This is why the national guidelines now recommend a booster dose for chickenpox before children go to kindergarten.

How are vaccines given?

There are three major ways vaccines are given. The first and most common is an injection through the skin. The vaccine is then deposited either into the underlying muscle (an intramuscular injection) or into the space just below the skin (a subcutaneous injection).

Injections through the skin obviously hurt but not in the way you might think. In my experience, children cry more when the fluid is injected *under* the skin than when the needle *pierces* the skin. This is why skin-numbing agents are less effective than parents hope against the immediate vaccine-injection pain; the agents only protect against the pain that occurs when the needle pierces the skin.

A second way to give vaccines is orally, or through the mouth. Though this method is less painful, there are few oral vaccines available. The rotavirus vaccine is currently the only one of the common childhood vaccines given orally. There was an oral polio vaccine available in the past, but because it had a very slight risk of actually causing polio, it has not been recommended in the United States since the year 2000.

A third method of administering vaccines is intranasally, or through a spray up the nose. One type of flu vaccine for older children and young adults can be given this way. Surprisingly, while some children prefer a nasal vaccine over a shot, many children detest the nasal method and prefer the injection if offered a choice.

What is a Vaccine Information Statement?

A Vaccine Information Statement (VIS) is a short (usually two-page) information sheet produced by the Centers for Disease Control and Prevention (CDC) that contains relevant information about a given vaccine. It usually contains a description of the disease the vaccine is protecting against, a description of the vaccine, recommendations about who should and should not receive the vaccine, and the potential risks of the vaccine. Healthcare providers who give certain vaccines are required to provide the individual or family with the appropriate VIS before each vaccine is given.

What are some common side effects of vaccines?

There are a number of common side effects of vaccines (see the following list). Some of these side effects occur in only one in one hundred recipients, while others occur in up to half of the recipients. Fortunately, not all of the side effects on the list occur with each vaccine; some only occur with a few vaccines. Even better, all of these side effects are mild and transient and are usually gone within two to three days. You can find the complete list of side effects for any given vaccine on the appropriate VIS at www.immunize.org/vis.

Common Vaccine Side Effects

- Soreness, redness, and swelling at the injection site
- Fever
- Headache
- Tiredness

- Loss of appetite
- Fussiness
- Vomiting, diarrhea, and abdominal pain
- Body aches
- Rash
- Itching
- Runny nose, nasal congestion, wheezing (from the intranasal influenza vaccine)

How can I prevent or manage minor side effects from vaccines?

The most common side effects of any vaccine are pain, soreness, and fever. Fortunately, those are the most treatable side effects as well. All three symptoms respond well to appropriate doses of acetaminophen (Tylenol) or ibuprofen (Motrin, Advil). In my experience, ibuprofen lasts longer, over six hours, and does a better job of reducing a high fever. However, ibuprofen is known to upset the stomach. Acetaminophen is easier on the stomach but requires dosing every four hours. Unless a child is vomiting or has stomach pain, I start with ibuprofen. If a child has stomach symptoms, though, I prefer to use acetaminophen. Aspirin is never recommended for children under the age of eight, due to an increased risk of liver complications.

Another reason I prefer ibuprofen over acetaminophen is that a study published in the fall of 2008 linked acetaminophen use to an increased risk for asthma. The study was published in a respected medical journal, *The Lancet*, and over two hundred thousand children were studied in thirty-one countries. This was a *huge* study; most medical studies contain fewer than a thousand participants. The results showed that children who received paracetamol (known as acetaminophen in the United States) in the first year of life had a higher risk of developing asthma by the time they were seven years old. In addition, the response was dose dependent, meaning that infants who used paracetamol more frequently had an increased risk of developing asthma when compared with children who received it only occasionally.

I am not using this study to always recommend against acetaminophen. As I said earlier, if a child is vomiting or has stomach pain, I prefer to use acetaminophen. And the risk was not extraordinarily high, only an increase of one and a half times the usual rate for occasional users of acetaminophen and three times the usual rate for frequent users. However, all things being equal, I do recommend ibuprofen over acetaminophen. Both do a good job of relieving pain and reducing fevers, and there was no association between ibuprofen and asthma in the *Lancet* study.

In my office, we always offer pain medication when we are giving vaccines to children. About half the parents like to give a dose of medicine before the vaccine is given. Their rationale is that they know vaccines usually hurt and don't want to delay treating the pain. Also, if you give the pain medicine far enough in advance of the injections, you have a better chance of the medicine controlling both the immediate pain of the injection as well as the sore muscle that occurs later on.

The other half of the parents are more concerned about giving unnecessary medicine to their children and prefer to wait to see if any pain relief is needed. For those parents concerned about the medication, I try to reassure them that with appropriate dosing, the medication is very safe in children.

How do you dose pain medication for children?

The dose of pain medication (acetaminophen or ibuprofen) is based solely on a child's weight, not his or her age. So I recommend ignoring the age categories on the dosing sheets, unless you have no idea how much your child weighs and don't have a scale in the house. (If you only have an adult scale available, weigh yourself with and without your child to approximate his or her weight.) For the appropriate dosage charts, look at the medicine bottle, the insert in the box, or these websites: http://www.babycenter.com/0_ acetaminophen-dosage-chart_11886.bc or http:// www.babyzone.com/baby_toddler_preschooler_ health/article/ibuprofen-dosage-chart or http://www. permanente.net/homepage/kaiser/pdf/3533.pdf.

For young children, you also need to be aware that there are two forms of liquid acetaminophen and ibuprofen: infant drops and children's suspension. The infant drops are more concentrated so that less volume of medicine needs to be given to little babies. However, if you are giving infant drops but mistakenly choose the volume from the children's suspension column of the table, you will give your baby an overdose. Overdoses of both acetaminophen and ibuprofen can be very serious, so be extra careful when managing liquid medicine for children.

What are some rare and/or more severe side effects of vaccines?

All vaccines, just like all medicines, have the risk of causing an allergic reaction. For example, you might be allergic to any one of the ingredients in the vaccine, such as the gelatin or preservative. Fortunately, severe allergic reactions that cause breathing or swallowing problems are very rare, occurring at an estimated rate of less than one in a million doses. In addition, these severe allergic reactions usually occur quickly, within minutes or maybe a few hours after the vaccine. So if you don't have a reaction by then, you are unlikely to have a severe allergic reaction at all.

There are a number of other severe reactions that are known to occur with certain vaccines. The DTaP VIS has listed some uncommon risks such as seizure (one child in fourteen thousand), nonstop crying for over three hours (one child in one thousand), and a high fever over 105°F (one child in sixteen thousand). While scary, these reactions are not noted to cause permanent damage. The chickenpox VIS also lists seizures as a risk (less than one child in one thousand) and pneumonia ("very rare").

The MMR VIS has several moderate risks listed. These include seizures (one child in three thousand) and temporary joint pain and stiffness (one out of every four recipients for teenage or adult women). It also lists thrombocytopenia, or a low platelet count, as a risk of the vaccine, occurring in one recipient in thirty thousand. Platelets are necessary to help your blood clot when you are cut, so low platelets can lead to a temporary bleeding disorder.

Another side effect that seems to be linked to some vaccines is Guillain-Barré syndrome (or GBS). GBS is an autoimmune syndrome in which the body's immune system attacks the body's own nerves. Without the use of certain nerves, your muscles will not function and paralysis sets in. In a population of people who have not recently received vaccines, GBS randomly occurs at a background rate of about one in a million people. (The background of a disease is the average rate the disease occurs over several years.)

In the 1970s, GBS was clearly linked to a specific type of flu vaccine, the swine flu vaccine. Interestingly, the actual risk only changed from a prevaccine rate of approximately one case of GBS in a million people to a postvaccine rate of eleven to twelve cases of GBS per million people. So even though you were eleven or twelve times more likely to develop GBS in the first six weeks after the swine flu vaccine, your actual risk of GBS was still very low, around one in one hundred thousand recipients of the vaccine.

GBS is less clearly linked to other vaccines, such as Tdap, the nasal influenza vaccine, and the meningitis vaccine. For example, several adolescents have had

GBS within a month of having received the meningitis vaccine, but it is not clear if the GBS is linked to the vaccine. Specifically, experts are unsure if the rate of GBS after that vaccine is higher than the one in a million background rate. As the meningitis vaccine is still new, more research and monitoring will need to be done before a better estimate of the risk of GBS is available.

Finally, the MMR and DTaP VIS mention that other serious problems have been reported after administration of the given vaccine. These problems include long-term seizures, coma, or lowered consciousness and permanent brain damage (both MMR and DTaP) and deafness (MMR only). These problems occur so rarely that it is difficult for experts to be sure if they are related to the vaccine or not.

You might notice that one problem I am not listing as a side effect of vaccines is autism. Despite concerns linking autism to both the MMR vaccine and to the thimerosal preservative in vaccines, in my opinion, the preponderance of the evidence does not show any connection. I discuss both of these theories in more detail in chapter 23.

Chapter 2

PRINCIPLES OF VACCINES

- What is the rationale for vaccinations for the average family?
- Are there reasons that vaccination might be more important to certain families?
- What is the rationale for vaccinations from a public health perspective?
- What is herd immunity?
- How can we compare the risks and benefits for individuals with those for society?
- What are some examples of a vaccine success story?
- What is an example of a vaccine that has mixed risks and benefits?
- What is an example of a vaccine that has not worked?

What is the rationale for vaccinations for the average family?

The major reason for vaccinating your child with a given vaccine is to protect your child from that specific disease. Thus, if your child gets the Haemophilus influenzae type B (HiB) vaccine, she is much less likely to ever get sick from HiB. Given that HiB is a terrible disease with a risk of meningitis and even death, most parents would like to prevent the illness if at all possible.

Another reason to vaccinate your child involves protecting other people who are close to your child. For example, rubella is a very mild, almost inconsequential disease for children. However, if a pregnant woman is infected with rubella during the first few months of pregnancy, there is a high risk of significant birth defects in the unborn child. So while you may not care if your child gets rubella, you certainly want to prevent your pregnant sister or neighbor from catching it from someone in your house.

Similarly, pertussis, or whooping cough, is a severe disease in infants but a milder disease in older children. Children less than six months old have not been fully immunized against pertussis and are more vulnerable. If you have a new baby in your house, you might want to make sure that your older children are vaccinated against whooping cough so that your newborn is not exposed.

Are there reasons that vaccination might be more important to certain families?

If an individual in the family has certain high-risk medical conditions, then vaccination might be even more important. For example, some children lack a functioning spleen due to genetic conditions, such as sickle cell disease, or from spleen surgery after a car accident. These children are at higher risk of becoming infected with certain bacteria such as HiB, pneumococcus, or meningococcus. In this circumstance, you would want to provide an extra level of protection with the appropriate vaccine.

Alternatively, someone in your family may have a weakened immune system from chemotherapy or certain medical conditions. Such a person would become much sicker than the average patient if he or she were to catch certain infections, and yet this person's compromised immune system might preclude vaccination. In this situation, close family members and other caretakers should be vaccinated in order to prevent passing infections on to the affected relative.

What is the rationale for vaccinations from a public health perspective?

There are several reasons that society recommends vaccinations. The simplest reason is that vaccines prevent disease, and thus, society as a whole has fewer illnesses. The more individuals who are vaccinated against chickenpox, the fewer cases of chickenpox will occur. This means there will be fewer days missed from school and work and fewer visits to doctors and hospitals, thus increasing the productivity of society.

In addition, while some people may be only annoyingly ill from a disease, others might suffer severe complications from the same disease. For example, some cases of chickenpox are much more severe than others. Adolescents and adults with chickenpox are more likely to develop pneumonia and require hospitalization. If there are fewer cases of chickenpox in a community due to mass vaccination, then there will also be fewer severe cases of chickenpox in the community.

Let's use a numerical example. If you have two million cases of chickenpox per year and one in every one thousand cases ends up in the hospital, you will have two thousand hospital admissions in a given year. However, if your vaccine decreases the number of cases by 95 percent (remember, no vaccine is perfect), then you will only have a hundred thousand cases of chickenpox and thus only a hundred hospital admissions. Immunizing society as a whole decreases the number of severe illnesses and hospitalizations associated with a disease.

Society also benefits from mass immunization because some individuals have medical reasons that prevent them from receiving a vaccine or that put them at a higher risk for complications if they get sick, such as having a suppressed immune system from chemotherapy. With fewer cases of chickenpox circulating in the community, there is a decreased risk that these immunosuppressed individuals will be exposed to the disease. This brings us to the concept of herd immunity.

What is herd immunity?

Herd immunity is the additional protection against a disease that a community acquires when the vaccination rate against that disease crosses a certain threshold.

Wow. That's quite a mouthful. Let me give an example and then try to explain the details of the concept.

Let's say that we immunize 92 percent of the population of a community against polio and that the vaccine is 100 percent effective. We might reasonably expect to see the number of cases of polio decrease by 92 percent, leaving the remaining 8 percent of cases for those people who were not vaccinated. However, in reality, the number of cases of polio decreases by over 99 percent. That extra 7 percent of protection is due to herd immunity.

Herd immunity is a major societal benefit of mass vaccinations. If enough members of a community are vaccinated and thus protected against a disease, then even if the disease reappears, it will only be able to spread to a few people. Because there are no longer very many susceptible hosts, the transmission of the disease will die out quickly. Furthermore, since most illnesses are passed from person to person, one unimmunized person living in a highly immunized community is unlikely to be exposed to any given disease. That unimmunized person is protected by the immunity of the herd of people around him.

For most illnesses, the estimated herd immunity threshold is a vaccination rate of around 90 percent. This means that if 90 percent of the population, or "herd," is successfully protected against the illness, the disease will die out because there aren't enough susceptible hosts to perpetuate its transmission.

Note that herd immunity does not require perfection. That's lucky—because no vaccine is 100 percent effective. In addition, not all children are vaccinated. Some children have medical exemptions against the vaccinations, and some parents refuse vaccinations for their children based on other reasons. However, if the number of vaccinated people is high enough, the disease is unlikely to resurface or cause an epidemic.

Of course, if the protection percentage drops too far below the herd immunity threshold, then the disease has room to spread and grow. Since no vaccine is 100 percent effective, the loss of herd immunity puts even vaccinated people at risk. In 1994 in the former Soviet Union, the collapse of the public health system led to decreased immunization rates and an epidemic of diphtheria. Whereas most developed countries might have less than twenty-five cases a year, the Soviet Union had almost forty thousand cases that year. Given the disease's 3 percent fatality rate, twelve hundred people died that year who might have lived had their national immunization program been up to date. In addition, over thirty-eight thousand people were sick, and possibly hospitalized, with the disease.

How can we compare the risks and benefits for individuals with those for society?

For many people, it helps to compare the public

health perspective on vaccines versus individual family choice by using an example with numbers. Imagine an illness named virus X that infects every child in the first year of life. While most children with virus X stay at home with a moderate fever and rash for seven to ten days, one in a thousand children develops the severe form of virus X, which requires a week of hospitalization. Some of those hospitalized children recover completely, some have significant developmental delays, and 20 percent die. Given that four million children are born in the United States every year, we would expect four thousand children to develop the severe version of virus X annually, of which eight hundred would die.

Now imagine we have a vaccine that prevents virus X and is 90 percent effective, meaning that 90 percent of children will develop antibodies and be protected if exposed to virus X. Of the four million children previously mentioned, 3,600,000 will be protected by the vaccine, and four hundred thousand will still be susceptible. Using the one in one thousand risk of severe disease, we would now only have four hundred children being hospitalized with the severe disease and only eighty children dying.

However, because of herd immunity, after a time, practically nobody gets virus X because it is not around to spread to other people. So in fact, while four hundred thousand children lack the antibodies even after vaccination, most don't get the disease. In fact, we might have only a hundred cases of virus X in the United States per year. Statistically, this means that we will see the severe disease only once every ten years and a death from the illness only once every fifty years. That is the benefit of herd immunity.

Now, nothing in life or medicine is perfect, including our virus X vaccine. We find that one in fifty thousand children has a severe reaction to the vaccine and is severely developmentally delayed, and 10 percent of those children die. That means that if four million kids are vaccinated each year, eighty children get a severe reaction, and eight children die.

So now you are a parent and have to make a decision about the vaccine for virus X. If the vaccine has just been introduced, you probably have heard of people in your community with the severe disease and probably want to vaccinate to protect against those severe complications.

However, forty years later, families are not aware of the severe version of virus X because it only happens in the whole United States once every ten years. More importantly, because it is so rare, the risk of severe illness from virus X is actually lower than the risk of adverse reaction to the vaccine. From a purely personal point of view, it is safer for your child to skip the vaccine.

On the other hand, from a public health point of view, if enough parents avoid the vaccine, then virus X will return, and ultimately more children will be harmed or will die from the illness than from the vaccine. In a very simplistic way, the public health assessment is that the vaccine, even when causing eighty severe reactions and eight deaths every year, is better than the reemergence of the illness.

Of course this is a simplistic scenario. What if there are more adverse reactions to the vaccine? Or unknown ones? What if the numbers are different? But to be fair, experts in international medicine see children die regularly of vaccine-preventable diseases. Yet even though they are highly publicized, severe vaccine reactions are extremely rare.

You may be surprised to know that virus X is not hypothetical. It actually has a name: measles. Before the vaccine was introduced, every child developed measles, one in a thousand children developed severe complications, and one in five thousand children died. However, because of herd immunity from the vaccine, we've had less than a hundred cases of measles in the United States in recent years, and most of those were imported from overseas. The only significant change I made in this scenario is modifying the risk of severe reactions to the vaccine. I chose one in fifty thousand for illustrative purposes. The quoted risk for encephalitis developing after the measles vaccine is one in two million, so the risk of serious side effects is actually much less than shown in our virus X example.

What are some examples of a vaccine success story?

The greatest vaccine success story of the modern age involves smallpox. Smallpox was a highly contagious viral illness that killed over 25 percent of those who were infected and left survivors maimed and disfigured. Fortunately, smallpox only infected humans, spread relatively slowly, and could be easily prevented by vaccination. Thus, it was possible to prevent the spread of the disease by immunizing enough people and quarantining affected individuals while contagious.

Starting in the 1960s, the World Health Organization (WHO) made a concerted effort to isolate epidemics of smallpox and vaccinate entire populations in the areas surrounding the epidemic. The number of cases of smallpox worldwide declined from estimates of over two million in the 1960s to zero by the late 1970s. In 1980, the WHO officially certified the world free of smallpox, and the vaccine is no longer given.

Another vaccine success story is polio. The number of cases of paralytic polio worldwide has decreased from three hundred thousand in the late 1980s to less than two thousand cases in the year 2006. This progress is mostly due to a global eradication program that began in 1988. Unfortunately, polio will be more difficult than smallpox to eradicate. The polio virus can cause not only the severe, paralytic form of the illness but also a milder, more common presentation. Most individuals with the milder form do not even know they have the disease and can thus continue to spread it to others through their bowel movements. In areas of poor sanitation, this is a common form of transmission.

What is an example of a vaccine that has mixed risks and benefits?

Rotavirus is a diarrhea-producing virus that mostly affects infants and leads to copious watery diarrhea. In the United States, because of good medical care, children almost never die from this illness. However, they often become dehydrated and are occasionally hospitalized. In 1998, an effective vaccine that decreased the severity of the illness as well as the number of hospitalizations it causes was approved after the normal review process.

But within several months of the introduction of the new vaccine, an increase in a rare bowel problem called intussusception was noted in children who had received the vaccine. The absolute increase in risk was only one in ten thousand children. However, given the fact that intussusceptions are life-threatening and sometimes require surgery, even that small an increase in the risk was enough to cause the CDC to pull the vaccine from the market in the United States.

Notice, however, that the analysis of the rotavirus vaccine depends almost entirely on the geographic location of each child. In the United States, where children rarely die of dehydration from diarrhea, the increased risk of intussusception far outweighs any concerns when compared with those associated with diarrhea.

However, outside the United States, over four hundred thousand children a year die from rotaviral diarrhea. For children in many countries, the risk of death from rotavirus far outweighs the risk of intussusception. If the vaccine was widely used in those countries, for every one child who dies from an intussusception, twenty or thirty children who otherwise would have died from the virus would now live because of the vaccine.

Of note, a different version of rotavirus vaccine was approved in 2006. So far it has the same benefits of the previous vaccine (decreased severity of illness and fewer hospitalizations), with no increased risk of intussusception. Given the history of the previous rotavirus vaccine and intussception, this new vaccine is being closely monitored.

What is an example of a vaccine that has not worked?

For many years, scientists have been trying to create a vaccine for HIV, the virus that leads to AIDS. Unfortunately, after twenty years of research, they are no closer to finding an effective vaccine than they were when they started. HIV is a unique virus that actually attacks a person's T cells so they are then unable to mount a counterattack. Given that current vaccine methods use a person's immune system to attack the invading organism, it appears that an HIV vaccine will need a novel method to work.

Chapter 3

A BRIEF HISTORY OF VACCINES

■ What is variolation?

■ Who was Edward Jenner and what did he achieve?

■ Why was Louis Pasteur famous for the rabies vaccine?

■ What vaccines became available in the early twentieth century?

■ What is the history of the flu vaccine?

■ What vaccines have become available in the last sixty years?

■ What is the future of vaccines?

What is variolation?

From the earliest eras of history, healers observed that if a person happened to survive a given illness the first time, he or she would not become ill if exposed to the same illness in the future. Specifically, people who contracted and then survived smallpox (variola) would not suffer the infection the next time a smallpox epidemic swept through the community. This concept led to the process of variolation, where scabs or pus from a person infected with smallpox would be introduced into another person. The hope was that this exposure would only induce a mild case of smallpox in the recipient and thus protect the recipient from a severe case of smallpox in the future.

There were several recorded methods of variolation. The first was to remove scabs from a person infected with smallpox, let them dry, and then grind them into a powder. That powder could either be inhaled by an uninfected person or introduced into the recipient's vein using a needle. Another method involved removing some pus and fluid from a smallpox blister and placing it under the skin of the recipient.

The origin of variolation is unclear, with different accounts stating that it occurred in China as early as 200 BC, AD 1100, and AD 1579. Whenever it began, variolation had progressed and spread across Asia in time to be common practice in the Ottoman Empire in 1716. It was in that year that the wife of the British ambassador, Lady Mary Wortley Montagu, observed physicians in Constantinople performing the procedure. She was sufficiently impressed to allow her own son to be inoculated.

After she returned to England in 1721, Lady Montagu had her daughter successfully inoculated against smallpox. This procedure caught the attention of the royal physician, and an experiment was planned. Several prisoners who were sentenced to death were offered the opportunity for freedom in exchange for undergoing variolation. All the prisoners survived. Within several years, the royal family of Britain and the royal families of many other countries underwent the procedure.

Variolation was never completely safe. While many recipients only had a mild case of smallpox, it was possible to develop a more severe case as well. Reports show that 1–2 percent of recipients actually died after the procedure. However, when compared to a mortality rate of 30 percent during a smallpox epidemic, it was felt to be a risk worth taking.

Who was Edward Jenner and what did he achieve?

Edward Jenner (1749–1823) was a British general physician who practiced in Berkeley, England. He had survived variolation as a child and was thus immune to smallpox. He was very learned, writing papers on medical matters, such as heart disease, as well as papers on natural history, such as how a new-born cuckoo bird was able to push his nest mates out of the nest. His most famous research, though, was on the prevention of smallpox by vaccination.

In rural Berkeley, where Jenner practiced, it was common knowledge that individuals who had experienced cowpox were protected from acquiring smallpox. Cowpox was a mild disease that caused blisters on a cow's teats. It could be spread to humans and was usually acquired by people when milking cows. Jenner postulated that if he were able to expose a person to cowpox, he could introduce this milder disease, which would then protect the individual from the more deadly smallpox.

Using his knowledge of variolation, on May 14, 1796, Jenner removed pus from the cowpox blister of a young woman, Sarah Nelmes. He then spread the pus over cuts in the skin of an eight-year-old boy, James Phipps, who had never had smallpox or cowpox. James developed a mild case of cowpox a week later and recovered uneventfully.

Six weeks later Jenner exposed James to the pus from a blister on a smallpox patient in the normal manner of variolation. James did not develop smallpox on this or subsequent exposures. The experiment had worked; introducing the cowpox illness could provide protection from subsequent smallpox exposure. Jenner named the process *vaccination*, which is derived from the Latin word *vacca*, meaning "cow."

Jenner reported this case and thirteen others to the Royal Society at the end of 1796. The medical establishment, as cautious as ever, was hesitant to accept the findings and recommended that he not publish his reports because it might injure his reputation. In 1798, Jenner published, at his own expense, a small book based on his case reports of his successful experiments on twenty-three people. The rather grand title of this publication was *An Inquiry into the Causes and Effects of the* Variolae Vaccinae, *a Disease Discovered in Some of the Western Counties of England, Particularly Gloucestershire, and Known by the Name of the Cowpox.*

Over the next several years, Jenner perfected his method of vaccination. He found a way to dry the material from a cowpox lesion so that it would not lose its effectiveness. By storing the dried material in a glass container, people were able to transmit the material around the world. By 1810, communities were being vaccinated with Jenner's dried cowpox lesions in Europe, India, and the newly formed United States of America.

It took over forty years for the medical community to fully embrace Jenner's findings. However, over time, it was clear that his method of vaccination was superior to variolation because of the lower risk of illness and death. In 1840, variolation was banned in Great Britain, and the vaccine was provided free of charge to those who wished it. In 1853, the smallpox vaccine was made mandatory by the age of three months, or the family would be fined. The era of compulsory vaccinations had begun.

Even though Jenner is appropriately credited with publishing the first paper on using cowpox to prevent smallpox, there were several other individuals who performed the procedure before Jenner. For example, Benjamin Jesty, a farmer from Dorset, England, inoculated his wife and children using cowpox in 1774, over twenty years before Jenner's experiment. Unfortunately, Jesty's wife developed a severe infection from the scratches introduced on her arm during the transmission of the cowpox pus and nearly died. While Jesty did inoculate some other relatives and neighbors, he did not widely disseminate the information, leaving it to Jenner to receive the credit.

Why was Louis Pasteur famous for the rabies vaccine?

Louis Pasteur (1822–1895) was a French chemist and biologist. He is most famous for his germ theory, which showed that most infections were due to microorganisms, and for the process of pasteurization, which uses heat and pressure to prevent the spoiling of food. In fact, he was one of the founders of the modern science of microbiology, which focuses on the biology of microorganisms.

Later in his career, Pasteur studied rabies, a lethal disease that even in the twenty-first century has no known cure. His studies showed that the microorganism that causes rabies, later known to be a virus, sequestered in the central nervous system. He then used the spinal cord of a rabid dog to induce the illness in other animals. Over time, he was able to weaken the virus, with the goal of using the attenuated virus as a vaccine.

In July 1885, Pasteur was able to test his vaccine on a human being. A young man named Joseph

Meister had been bitten by a rabid dog and was sure to die. Pasteur was able to treat him with his attenuated virus and saved his life. Over the subsequent years, Pasteur's treatment saved the lives of thousands of others.

What vaccines became available in the early twentieth century?

Several vaccines were developed in the late 1800s and early 1900s. Waldemar Haffkine, a Russian microbiologist who spent much of his time in India, developed a vaccine for cholera in 1892 and a vaccine for bubonic plague in 1897. Given the millions of people who have died over the centuries from these diseases, these two achievements should have made him as famous as Edward Jenner, but he is relatively unknown outside the field of immunology. The cholera vaccine was recently updated into an oral vaccine, but it is not recommended by the CDC and is not available in the United States. The plague vaccine is no longer commercially available in the United States.

An early version of the typhoid vaccine was developed around the turn of the century by Almorth Wright, a British bacteriologist. His work was taken up in the United States by Frederick Russell, an officer in the U.S. Army. In 1911, the typhoid vaccine became mandatory in the army, and illness and death rates dropped dramatically in just two years.

Diphtheria was a major killer in the late 1800s and early 1900s. Interestingly, the first step toward a cure for diphtheria was not a vaccine but rather the development of a diphtheria antitoxin. This antitoxin, when given after someone became sick with diphtheria, was able to halt or reverse the effects of the toxin released by the diphtheria bacteria and saved thousands of lives. In fact, the Iditarod, the famous annual dogsled race in Alaska, commemorates an over six-hundred-mile dogsled run to deliver diphtheria antitoxin to Nome, Alaska, which prevented a diphtheria epidemic.

Emil von Behring won the first Nobel Prize in Medicine for his research into diphtheria antitoxin. A diphtheria vaccine became available in the 1920s and slowly spread around the world. The death rate in the United States dropped from thousands of deaths per year in the 1920s to virtually zero by the 1950s.

The first whole-cell pertussis vaccine was developed in the 1930s. It was combined with the diphtheria vaccine and the tetanus vaccine (developed in the 1920s) to create the DTP vaccine. This vaccine stayed in use for almost fifty years. Other vaccines that were developed in the first half of the twentieth century include the bacille Calmette-Guérin (BCG) vaccine against tuberculosis and the yellow fever vaccine, both of which are still in use today.

What is the history of the flu vaccine?

In 1918, the influenza, or flu, virus infected over 20 percent of the world's population and lead to over twenty million deaths. The United States alone had five hundred thousand deaths. This pandemic (an epidemic across continents or of worldwide proportions) was caused by a sudden shift in the antigens on the influenza virus. Usually the flu antigens change gradually in a process called antigenic drift. This allows people to retain some protection against the flu because they have seen some of the antigens before.

However, if the antigens change suddenly, in a process called antigenic shift, then the virus is effectively a new disease because people have no past immunity to the new antigens. Whenever antigenic shift occurs, more people will become ill, and the disease will spread more widely. There have been several pandemics in the past, and the World Health Organization is currently preparing for the next one.

The first flu vaccine was developed in the 1940s, with newer versions, such as the intranasal flu vaccine, developed since then. The recommendations for receiving the flu vaccine have broadened over time. The vaccine used to be reserved for people over age sixty-five or with chronic medical conditions. In the past ten years, the recommendations have expanded to include adults over age fifty, then children under age two, then children under five, and now all children between six months and eighteen years of age.

One interesting historical note involves the swine flu vaccine of 1976–77. The experts were concerned that this particular flu would be the next pandemic and strongly recommended the widespread distribution of the vaccine across the United States. Unfortunately, the vaccine had the rare but serious side effect of causing Guillain-Barré syndrome (GBS) in one out of every one hundred thousand recipients (as compared to the background population rate of one in a million people). Even though it was a rare side effect, the mass vaccination program was halted in midwinter.

What vaccines have become available in the last sixty years?

The last sixty years have seen the development of the majority of vaccines discussed in this book. These include both the injectable killed polio vaccine developed by Jonas Salk as well as the live, attenuated oral polio vaccine developed by Albert Sabin. (Remember that a killed vaccine has no risk of transmitting the disease to the vaccine recipient, while an attenuated vaccine is merely weakened and rarely can transmit the actual disease.) Together, these two vaccines decreased the incidence of polio in the United States from over fifty thousand cases to fewer than two hundred in just twelve years.

Salk's vaccine was the first used in mass vaccination campaigns in the 1950s but was replaced by the Sabin vaccine in the 1960s because the oral vaccine was easier to administer and provided longer-lasting immunity. However, because the oral vaccine was a live (attenuated) vaccine, it had a rare risk of causing polio and full-blown paralysis. For this reason, the oral vaccine was replaced with the injectable vaccine in 2000.

The measles, mumps, and rubella vaccines were introduced in the 1960s and combined into one vaccine in the early 1970s. At first, just one dose of the measles vaccine was recommended, but despite a 95 percent protection rate, epidemics still occurred. It appeared that measles was so contagious that the threshold for herd immunity was higher than

95 percent. Since the second MMR was recommended in the 1980s, the level of protection has increased to over 99 percent, and measles has become a very rare disease in the United States. Not only has the incidence of measles decreased, but the incidence of congenital rubella syndrome dropped from twenty thousand cases in the mid-1960s to fewer than fifty cases a year since 2000.

Also during these two decades, the United Nations put forth a heroic effort to eradicate smallpox from the world. Over the twenty years from 1959 to 1979, smallpox vaccination and quarantine efforts were successful in reducing the number of cases. By 1980, the United Nations declared that the first virus in history had been completely contained and no longer caused human disease.

In the 1980s and the 1990s, several vaccines were approved in rapid succession. The meningitis, hepatitis B, and pneumococcal vaccines were approved in the 1980s, while the HiB, DTaP, chickenpox, and hepatitis A vaccines were approved in the 1990s. The first rotavirus vaccine was approved in the mid-1990s but removed from the market due to side effects just a few years later.

Since 2000, a pneumococcal vaccine for infants, a live, attenuated flu vaccine, two other rotavirus vaccines, and the first human papillomavirus vaccine have all been approved. In addition, several combination vaccines were also approved. The combination vaccines are important because with the large number of recommended vaccines for children, it is possible for a child to receive six injections at one well-child checkup. Even with the combination vaccines, an average two-month-old child will receive three injections and one oral vaccine at his or her well-child checkup.

What is the future of vaccines?

There are a number of areas of ongoing research in the field of vaccination. One area is the search for a vaccine for malaria. In 2005, the Bill and Melinda Gates Foundation donated over $250 million for research and development in this area. The foundation also donated over $300 million for HIV research, including research into developing a vaccine for HIV. Unfortunately, both these diseases have evolved ingenious methods of avoiding the immune system, and it may be a long time before effective vaccines become available.

One disease that is not as well known as HIV or malaria, but where a vaccine may soon become available, is group B streptococcus. Several promising vaccine studies are currently underway. Group B strep affects two main groups of people: pregnant women, who are able to pass the infection onto their babies during labor, and the elderly who have chronic medical conditions. If a newborn baby develops group B strep from the labor process, it is usually a severe infection that can lead to pneumonia, meningitis, and even death. In the elderly, severe group B strep infections affect thousands of people in the United States with a fatality rate of 10–40 percent.

Chapter 4

VACCINATION LOGISTICS

- Where can I find the most up-to-date vaccine schedules?
- What is the normal vaccination schedule for children and adults?
- Why are some vaccines given multiple times?
- Can you check to see if you have antibodies to a given disease to see if booster doses are necessary?
- Why do infants require so many booster doses?
- When should I defer or avoid getting a vaccine?
- What are some other rules about the timing of vaccine administration?
- What is the effect on the immune system when getting multiple vaccinations at once?
- Is it better to get the vaccinations in a group or to spread them out?
- What should I do if my child suffers from a significant problem after receiving a vaccine?
- What is the Vaccine Injury Compensation Program (VICP)?
- What is a vaccine registry?
- Do I have to give my children vaccines, or can I get an exemption?
- What are the pros and cons of religious and personal vaccine exemptions?

Where can I find the most up-to-date vaccine schedules?

The most up-to-date vaccination schedules can be found on the Internet at http://www.cdc.gov/nip/recs/child-schedule.htm for children and at http://www.cdc.gov/vaccines/recs/schedules/adult-schedule.htm for adults. In addition, you can look at http://www.cdc.gov/vaccines/spec-grps/default.htm for information pertinent to other specific groups, such as college students or pregnant women.

What is the normal vaccination schedule for children and adults?

Every year, the CDC prints out a recommended vaccine schedule for children and adults, complete with a full page of footnotes and explanations (see the links in the previous answer). However, this recommended schedule contains a number of acceptable variations. While the individual vaccines on the schedule are fixed, the number of booster doses is different in certain circumstances, and the timing of administration of the vaccines can vary by several months.

One factor in this variability depends on which brand of vaccine is being used. For example, with one brand of HiB vaccine, the six-month booster dose is necessary, but with another brand, the booster dose is not required.

Another variable factor in the vaccine schedule is that some vaccines have a specific recommended age for administration, but other vaccines have a recommended range of ages for when the vaccine should be given. For example, the first and second doses of the polio vaccine are recommended to be given at two and four months of age, respectively, while the third dose can be given at any time between six and eighteen months.

Finally, the availability of combination vaccines, where multiple vaccines are combined in one syringe, might affect the schedule. If hepatitis B was given separately, then the three doses could be given at birth, at one or two months, and at six months. However, hepatitis B is part of a combination vaccine along with polio and DTaP, both of which are recommended at four months of age. If you choose this combination vaccine at four months, you may be giving your child an extra dose of hepatitis B vaccine (which does not appear to be harmful). If you choose to avoid the extra dose of hepatitis B vaccine, you have to give polio and DTaP separately, which means two needles for your baby instead of just one needle with the combination vaccine.

With all this in mind, I am presenting the recommended vaccine schedule as given in my office
during the fall of 2008. You will see that we give a
hepatitis B dose at the four-month checkup, mainly
because we feel that fewer needles is more important
than avoiding the extra dose of hepatitis B. Other
offices might choose a slightly different schedule, but
as long as they are following the basic CDC recommendations, they will all be equally acceptable.

Recommended Vaccine Schedule
for Children

Birth:	Hepatitis B
2 months:	HiB, DTaP, pneumococcal, rotavirus, polio, hepatitis B
4 months:	HiB, DTaP, pneumococcal, rotavirus, polio, hepatitis B
6 months:	HiB, DTaP, pneumococcal, rotavirus, polio, hepatitis B, flu*
Every October:	Flu*
12 months:	MMR, chickenpox, hepatitis A, pneumococcal, HiB**
18 months:	DTaP, hepatitis A

4 to 6 years:	DTaP, polio, MMR, chicken-pox
11 to 12 years:	Meningitis, human papillo-mavirus (HPV)***, Tdap

* The flu vaccine is recommended at the six-month well-child checkup, if that visit falls during flu season (October through March), and every subsequent October for all children over the age of six months. The recommendation has recently been extended to administer the flu vaccine to all children under age eighteen. The flu vaccine can be given either as an injection (over age six months) or as a nasal spray (over age two years). In general, the first year children receive the vaccine, they should receive two doses a month apart.

**There is a shortage of the HiB vaccine in 2008. This has led to a temporary recommendation of not giving the HiB booster if a child has received the primary HiB series. When the shortage is relieved, we will start giving the vaccine at the twelve-month well-child checkup again and will also offer catch-up doses to those children who did not receive the twelve-month dose.

***The HPV vaccine is for women only and is given in a series of three doses.

In addition to this schedule, there are some additional recommendations for certain high-risk children. For example, the meningitis vaccine can be given as early as age two years if a child is at higher risk of developing that illness, such as a child with sickle cell disease. And if a child has a cochlear implant and is at high risk of pneumococcal disease, he or she can receive a different brand of the pneumococcal vaccine after age two, in addition to the pneumococcal vaccine given to infants.

The vaccine schedule for adults can be broken into two categories: vaccine by age and vaccine by risk. While some vaccines are fixed at certain ages, other vaccines are recommended only for certain high-risk situations. In addition, if adults did not receive certain vaccines as children, such as the MMR or chickenpox vaccines, they should be given catch-up doses as adults.

Recommended Vaccine Schedule for Adults

Age 9 to 26:	HPV (women only, series of 3 doses)
Age 50+:	Annual flu vaccine every October
Age 60:	Shingles vaccine once

Age 65:	Pneumococcal vaccine once
Every 10 years:	Td (but replace Td with Tdap once if younger than age 65)

For adults, the following vaccines are recommended in certain high-risk situations: flu, pneumococcal, hepatitis A, hepatitis B, and meningitis. Notice that the flu and pneumococcal vaccines are repeated in both the high-risk-group list and the vaccine-by-age list. This is because both of these vaccines are recommended not only when a person reaches a certain age but also at a younger age with certain medical conditions.

Why are some vaccines given multiple times?

When a vaccine dose is repeated, it is called a booster dose. A booster dose is used to enhance the body's immune response to a given disease. Even though the memory B and T cells are long lived, they will slowly disappear over time. This might be months or years depending on the disease, but over time, the immunity against that infection fades.

However, when the body sees a vaccine a second time, the memory B and T cells do two things. First, they make the necessary plasma cells and helper and killer T cells to restimulate the immune system. Second, they make extra copies of the memory B and T cells. Extra copies mean that it will take longer for all the memory cells for a certain infection to die off and it will take longer for immunity to that disease to fade away.

Another reason a booster dose is sometimes required is that studies have shown that for certain vaccines, a single dose is not enough to provide protection to the majority of recipients. For example, after one dose of hepatitis B vaccine, only about 60 percent of recipients produce sufficient antibodies to be protected. After two doses, the number of protected recipients increases to over 85 percent, and by the third dose, over 98 percent of recipients are protected. Because different people react differently, some people need an additional stimulus to provide a protective response. That additional stimulus comes in the form of a booster dose.

Can you check to see if you have antibodies to a given disease to see if booster doses are necessary?

Actually, you can draw blood and see if you have appropriate antibody levels for a given disease. I have a few families in my practice who prefer to follow this path instead of subjecting their children to additional vaccines, and so far the schools have accepted the results as proof of immunity.

However, this is an expensive process, especially if you are drawing blood for multiple diseases. And if the antibody levels are not high enough to prove immunity, the child still needs the vaccine, and thus will receive two needle pokes instead of just one. Finally, the goal of booster doses is to produce more memory B and T cells to make the immunity last longer. Even if your child is immune now, that doesn't guarantee that he or she will be immune five years from now. However, if your child receives a booster dose, he or she is more likely to have long-lasting immunity.

Why do infants require so many booster doses?

Unfortunately, some vaccines are not as effective in infants as they are in older children. For example, if the HiB vaccine is given to infants, you need a series of two or three doses to provide adequate protection. However, if the HiB vaccine was not given to an infant but is then given to a child over fifteen months of age, a single dose will provide sufficient protection. That said, HiB meningitis is more common and more dangerous in infants than in toddlers. So even though the HiB vaccine is not as effective in infants, we still want to give them as much protection as possible, and we do that by using booster doses.

A major reason vaccines are not as effective in infants is that a baby's immune system already has some protection from these diseases. At the end of her pregnancy, a mother transfers a complete set of her antibodies across the placenta and shares them with her baby. This set includes antibodies to any illness or disease to which the mother has been exposed, plus any antibodies from vaccines the mother has received. Note that the mother does not share the B cells that make the antibodies, merely the antibodies themselves.

These antibodies last for several months but are then slowly degraded by the baby's body. While they are present, though, they can interfere with the baby's own immune system. For example, if the baby's body already has antibodies to polio, its body is not as primed to make extra copies of the necessary B cells. However, when the maternal antibodies fade, the baby will no longer be protected. For this reason, infants are more likely to need a repeated stimulus to produce the necessary level of memory cells needed for long-lasting protection.

When should I defer or avoid getting a vaccine?

There are certain circumstances when you should not receive a given vaccine, either temporarily or permanently. Most of these situations are obvious. If you have ever had a severe allergic reaction to a vaccine in the past, you should never get another dose of that vaccine. Similarly, if after receiving a certain vaccine, you or your child had one of the other rare or severe reactions listed in chapter 1, you will probably want to avoid that vaccine in the future, unless you and your doctor agree that the benefits outweigh the risks of a repeat reaction.

Some people have other allergies that also preclude certain vaccinations. If you have ever had a severe allergic reaction to eggs, you should not receive the influenza vaccine. Similarly, if you have had a severe reaction to any one of the ingredients in a vaccine, such as yeast, gelatin, latex, or certain antibiotics, then you should never receive a vaccine with that ingredient. Please inform your doctor of any allergies before receiving any vaccines. The complete list of ingredients can be found in the package insert of a given vaccine. Your doctor should have a copy in his or her office, or you can find the information on the Internet.

Some other illnesses or chronic conditions preclude the use of certain vaccines. If you have asthma, other significant lung disease, heart disease, or diabetes, or if you are on long-term aspirin therapy, you should not receive the nasal influenza vaccine. Instead, people with the listed chronic conditions should be protected with the injectable flu vaccine. One reason for this recommendation is that there is an increased risk of wheezing after the nasal flu vaccine.

If individuals have had Guillain-Barré syndrome (GBS) in the past, they should not receive the nasal influenza vaccine. They also will want to discuss the matter with their physician and might not want to get the injectable influenza or meningitis vaccine either. There is some concern that these vaccines are associated with a higher risk of recurring GBS.

If your child has an unstable, progressive neurological disorder, you should discuss the benefits and risk of the DTaP or Tdap vaccine with your doctor before giving them to your child. However, a stable neurological disorder, such as cerebral palsy or even seizures, is not a reason to avoid those vaccines.

Immune deficiencies also require care with vaccinations. A weakened immune system might be caused by cancers such as leukemia, infections such as AIDS, or chemotherapy or radiation therapy. Certain medications, such as steroids, and certain other medical treatment, such as blood transfusions or gamma globulin injections, can also temporarily alter the immune system. In all these situations, there are complicated rules as to when, if ever, to vaccinate with certain vaccines, and you will need to discuss these rules with your doctor.

Pregnant women should not be vaccinated with the human papillomavirus or any live virus vaccines such as the MMR, varicella, shingles, or nasal influenza vaccine. Although the risk is theoretical, it is possible that the weakened virus could cause an infection in the mother that would then spread to the fetus. For similar reasons, the injectable polio vaccine is usually avoided during pregnancy but can be given in certain circumstances. There are no reasons to avoid any vaccines while breast-feeding.

If you have a moderate or severe illness at the time the vaccine is scheduled to be given, you should usually defer the vaccine until you have recovered. Unfortunately, I cannot find a good definition of "moderate illness." However, the following illnesses are considered only a mild illness, and vaccines may still be given: diarrhea, ear infections, and upper respiratory infections with or without a low-grade fever. In my office, I usually recommend deferring vaccines for fevers over 102°F.

What are some other rules about the timing of vaccine administration?

Vaccines should usually be given at the recommended ages and intervals, not earlier or later. The recommendations are derived from studies of measured antibody levels after vaccines were given at different ages, with the goal of providing the highest possible level of protection. So, for example, the HiB vaccine should not be given before six weeks of age and the rotavirus vaccine should not be given after thirty-two weeks of age.

In addition, many vaccines have recommended intervals between the original shots and the booster vaccines. The hepatitis A vaccine booster should be given more than six months after the original vaccine injection. There are rare exceptions to the rules (such as giving the measles vaccine to a child traveling to certain parts of the world), but those are clearly laid out in guidelines available to your doctor.

In addition, certain live-virus vaccines, such as MMR, varicella, shingles, nasal influenza, and yellow fever, have particular rules about how to space the vaccinations. Studies show that if two vaccines in this group are given on the same day or are given more than twenty-eight days apart, the resulting antibody levels are equivalent. However, if the two vaccines are given less than four weeks apart, the antibody response to the second vaccine is diminished, leading to suboptimal protection.

What is the effect on the immune system when getting multiple vaccinations at once?

Many parents worry that receiving multiple vaccines at the same time is stressful for a child. They frequently tell me that they are worried about overwhelming their child's immune system with so many different antigens, or foreign products. When I talk about stimulating the body to produce protective antibodies, they worry about overstimulating the immune system.

Fortunately, there is no evidence that this is true. On the most basic level, studies are commonly done to compare the antibody level when a vaccine is given alone to when it is given in combination with other vaccines. Studies are also done to see if the timing between different vaccines is relevant. For example, if vaccines are not given at the same time, do they need to be given a day or a week or a month apart? With very few exceptions, there is no difference in protection. This means that, from the body's point of view, a single-dose vaccine produces the same level of protective antibodies as a combination vaccine, and the spacing between vaccines is irrelevant. (An exception to this rule with regard to live, attenuated viral vaccines needing to be at least four weeks apart was discussed earlier.)

On a broader level, the immune system is very flexible. You should remember from chapter 1 that there are billions of B cell and helper T cell receptors ready to match almost any antigen in the world. The antigens in the vaccine are not catching the body unawares.

Finally, the volume of antigens in vaccines is not overwhelming. Even without vaccines, a baby is exposed to hundreds of new antigens on a daily basis, and the immune system is able to respond to all of them. Every new object that goes into the mouth provides several new antigens, whether it is food, a toy the dog slobbered on, or dirt from under the couch. And there are normal illnesses in the community to which the baby is exposed. Each new virus has several new antigens, and a strep throat has over twenty.

In contrast, the average vaccine has twenty to thirty antigens—well within the normal daily limit. It is true that the total of all the recommended vaccines at the two-, four-, and six-month well-child checkups is around 150 antigens. However, in comparison, that is the same order of magnitude as the normal daily exposure to antigens, and yet we don't worry about "overwhelming" the immune system with normal daily activities.

Is it better to get the vaccinations in a group or to spread them out?

In the end, it is best to simply get the vaccines in whatever way makes you most comfortable with your decision. From a public health viewpoint, it is best to get as many children vaccinated as quickly as possible. That not only builds up herd immunity but also protects each individual child from the various illnesses sooner. So the public health experts regularly encourage primary care physicians to vaccinate early and vaccinate often. They want us to not miss any opportunity to keep a child on schedule or to help a child catch up on immunizations.

However, if you are worried about giving multiple vaccines at once, it is better to spread them out than to not give them at all. Some parents worry about overwhelming the immune system and want to minimize any extra antigens on any given day. Some parents want to test each vaccine by itself to see if their child has a particular reaction. If several vaccines are given at the same time and the child has a fever of 104°F, the parent doesn't know which vaccine caused the problem.

I have my own personal example of the decision-making process for choosing a vaccine schedule. I am a "lumper" who liked to give clusters of vaccines so that my child only cried once. My wife was one of those parents who didn't want to overwhelm our children with too many vaccines at once. Together, we compromised on a schedule that only gave our children two injections at any one time. Our schedule prioritized what I considered the most important vaccines for the early checkups and put off the other recommended vaccines until subsequent visits. We also chose combination vaccines when available to minimize the total number of needle sticks our children had to receive.

My patients have created some other unusual schedules. Some parents give the first set of vaccines one at a time but the second set two at a time. If there have been no reactions up to that point, they are comfortable with giving the third set of vaccines at the six-month well-child checkup all at the same time. These parents figure that if their children haven't had a reaction yet, they probably won't in the future.

My most memorable vaccine schedule is from a mother who believes in only giving vaccines one at a time. She also breaks down all the combination vaccines into separate components when possible. So she gives one vaccine at the two-month well-child checkup and then comes in every week for five weeks to given the remaining five vaccines. She repeats the cycle after the four- and six-month well-child checkups. Even though I don't agree with her reasoning, I have to admire her dedication to her beliefs.

What should I do if my child suffers from a significant problem after receiving a vaccine?

The first thing to do is to contact your doctor. He or she will want to manage the immediate event, whether it is a seizure, a high fever, or just crying for several hours. The doctor might need to see your child in the office or the emergency room and, in severe cases, admit your child to the hospital.

After the immediate problem is stabilized, you and your doctor should discuss which vaccines were given and make a plan for future vaccinations. In some cases, a substitute vaccine will be suggested. For example, if a child is diagnosed with encephalopathy within seven days of receiving a DTaP vaccine, then that child should never receive a vaccination containing pertussis again. However, the DT vaccine will presumably be safe to finish the diphtheria and tetanus series.

Unfortunately, with combination vaccines and multiple vaccines given at once, it might be difficult to identify which vaccine was the likely culprit for the high fever. In that case, you might decide to give fewer vaccines at once for the next set of vaccines in the series. That way if you have a repeat episode of the high fever, then you can identify which vaccine might be to blame.

You should also recognize that the vaccine might not be the cause of the problem. Children have fevers and seizures all the time without any recent vaccinations. It could just be a coincidence that the two events occurred in the same few hours or days.

Finally, either you or your physician should report the event to the Vaccine Adverse Event Reporting System (VAERS). Information about VAERS can be found at http://vaers.hhs.gov/. You do not have to prove that the vaccine caused the problem. The researchers at VAERS simply want to know about any medical issues that occurred in close proximity to receiving vaccines. You can fill out the VAERS information online or print out a form and mail it to the organization.

Since 1990, the VAERS program has received well over a hundred thousand reports of medical events after vaccines. Over 85 percent of the reports are for mild and/or transient problems, such as fever, pain, or mild irritability. The remaining 15 percent include more serious experiences, such as being admitted to the hospital or requiring surgery.

If a pattern of events is seen with a given vaccine, then the FDA and CDC can act on the information. This is what occurred in the late 1990s with the rotavirus vaccine. Infants who recently received the rotavirus vaccine were suffering from an increased risk of intussusception, a bowel problem that usually requires surgery, at a higher rate than expected. After the first reports came in, the CDC launched a full investigation and subsequently recommended that the vaccine not be used in the United States.

What is the Vaccine Injury Compensation Program (VICP)?

During the 1970s, several vaccine manufacturers withdrew from the vaccine market due to financial and legal concerns. On the financial side, vaccines have never been a big money maker for a pharmaceutical company. The profit margin on vaccines has never approached that of certain categories of drugs, such as cholesterol-lowering medication. On the legal side, many companies were sued by parents who felt that a particular vaccine caused a particular injury to their child. Sometimes the medical explanations provided by the parents and their lawyers were at odds with the data from studies. After a court awarded a million-dollar judgment against a pharmaceutical company, the final vaccine manufacturers were poised to leave the market.

In 1986, President Reagan signed the National Childhood Vaccine Injury Act, which created the VICP. One goal of the VICP was to provide an alternative mechanism to the civil court system for evaluating whether or not a given injury was related to the administration of a given vaccine. If evidence was found, then the family would be compensated for the injury using funds collected by charging a tax on each vaccine sold. In essence, the VICP is a no-fault alternative for vaccine injuries.

One provision of this law is that families almost always have to file a claim with the VICP before they can sue a pharmaceutical company in civil court. This effectively sets up a large barrier to civil lawsuits because the parents need to go through the VICP process before they can sue the vaccine manufacturer. This provision is meant to discourage frivolous lawsuits while at the same time compensating families much more quickly if the injury is vaccine related.

The VICP has a table of severe injuries that are always presumed due to a vaccine and thus will always be compensated. Those injuries include an immediate life-threatening reaction to a vaccine (anaphylaxis), encephalopathy after an MMR or pertussis-containing vaccine, and vaccine-associated paralytic polio from the oral polio vaccine (which is no longer used in the United States).

In 2001, the VICP began receiving requests for compensation from parents based on claims that the MMR vaccine specifically, or the thimerosal in vaccines in general, contributed to the development of autism in their children. By 2008, the VICP had received over five thousand claims of this type.

After much discussion, the VICP decided to allow some test cases to move forward to special hearings to decide if the claims had merit. In 2007 and 2008, those hearings began, and the findings of those hearings are expected in 2008 or 2009. See page 84 for more information. Of note, the case of Hannah Poling, discussed in chapter 23, was one of those test cases. It was later settled, and the claim was withdrawn when the VICP agreed that the vaccines could plausibly be linked to her underlying mitochondrial disorder.

What is a vaccine registry?

A vaccine registry is a list of children and which vaccines they have received. A registry may be kept by a medical practice, a school, a health department, an individual state, several states in a region, or by the federal government. Depending on which organization is maintaining the registry, it may be mandatory or voluntary for the vaccine provider to report the vaccine to the registry.

In many ways, a vaccine registry is an electronic version of a child's immunization record. It maintains all the vaccine information in one place and makes it easier for parents to keep track of their child's vaccines without having to worry about losing that special piece of paper that has the shot record on it. In addition, if the registry is set up to allow other organizations to view the record, it can make it easier for schools and colleges to verify that the vaccines necessary for enrollment were given.

However, some parents object to the vaccine registry as an invasion of their child's medical privacy. They feel that medical decisions should not be public knowledge. Even if the registry is kept confidential and only allows access to certain organizations, some parents worry that the information is accessible to hackers who might do some mischief.

Whatever you think about vaccine registries, you need to be aware that they are becoming more and more common. Many states have already set up their own registries, and some groups of states have combined their state registries to form a regional vaccine registry. I fully expect that in the next twenty years, there will be a national vaccine registry.

Do I have to give my children vaccines, or can I get an exemption?

In general, the answer to this question is no, you don't have to give your child vaccines. I don't know of any law that requires you to give your child vaccines or risk having your child taken away from you for neglect. I have seen circumstances where a failure to vaccinate a child has become an issue in custody cases or in adoption proceedings. However, in general, the state will not interfere with your medical decisions for your child.

On the other hand, all states require that a child be vaccinated before attending school. Different states may have slightly different requirements, but most closely follow the CDC recommendations. So if you want your child to attend school (or preschool or day care in some states), you need to either vaccinate your child or obtain some sort of exemption.

All states allow medical exemptions. A medical exemption is when a doctor writes a letter explaining the medical reason a vaccine or vaccines should not be given. Most medical exemptions are usually narrowly based and only cover some vaccines. There are very rare medical circumstances where no vaccines should be given, but you don't want your child to be sick enough to justify that.

In addition to medical exemptions, there are also religious and personal exemptions, in which parents write a letter explaining their religious or personal beliefs that preclude the use of all or some vaccines. As of September 2008, forty-eight states allowed religious exemptions for vaccines. The two states that do not allow religious exemptions to vaccines are Mississippi and West Virginia. The most common example of a religion that opposes vaccines is the First Church of Christ, Scientist, otherwise known as the Christian Scientists.

Twenty-one states allow exemptions from vaccines based on an individual's or a parent's personal beliefs only, without regard to religious beliefs. This gives parents the option to pick and choose the vaccines they feel are best suited for their children, instead of following all the national recommendations. As of the fall of 2008, the twenty-one states that allow personal exemptions are Arkansas, Arizona, California, Colorado, Idaho, Louisiana, Maine, Michigan, Minnesota, New Hampshire, New Mexico, North Dakota, Ohio, Oklahoma, Oregon, Pennsylvania, Texas, Utah, Vermont, Washington, and Wisconsin. (For more information on vaccine exemptions for day cares and schools in various states, visit http://www.vaccinesafety.edu/)

Note that most people consider the religious exemption an all-or-nothing exemption. It is hard to argue that a given religion opposes some vaccinations but not others. This makes it difficult for parents in states with only a religious exemption to pick and choose vaccines based on their personal beliefs. In my practice in New York, a state that allows a religious but not a personal exemption, most families who choose not to vaccinate either request a religious exemption or homeschool their children.

What are the pros and cons of religious and personal vaccine exemptions?

One positive aspect of religious and personal vaccine exemptions is the implicit support for individual autonomy, a strong cultural value in the United States. Allowing exemptions means that families are free to choose, based on their personal beliefs, what goes into their own and their children's bodies, without interference from the state.

Many other countries do not place such value on family independence. When I asked a friend born in France what the average French family would do if required to vaccinate its children, he was a bit puzzled by the question. He implied that everyone in France would follow the rules and that no one would dream of not vaccinating his or her child. The value of the public good outweighs individual choice.

A very real, negative aspect of allowing various vaccine exemptions is that it decreases herd immunity. If more people are not vaccinated, there are more susceptible hosts for a given disease, and thus, the illness is able to spread more widely. Studies are very clear that there is a higher incidence of various vaccine-preventable diseases in states with personal vaccine exemptions than in states with only religious exemptions.

So the question our country continues to grapple with is this: At what point is it appropriate for society, in the interest of public health, to overrule an individual family's choice about vaccination?

As you have already noticed in this book, I am very much in favor of vaccines, but I am also very much in favor of parental choice. In a way, this reflects the two hats I wear on a daily basis. When I am a family physician, taking care of an entire family, I am that family's advocate. My goal is to support that family in its decision-making process and respect its final decision, even if I don't agree.

However, I am also a doctor in a small town of fifty thousand, and I know how the child with pertussis in my office today affects the community. I see that disease being spread to other unvaccinated children. So far I have not had to admit a baby with pertussis to the hospital, but if that ever happens, I will know that part of the reason that baby is in the intensive care unit is that there are a large number of unvaccinated children in my community.

In my opinion, at the present time in the United States, with a minimal presence for most vaccine-preventable diseases, I still strongly support parental choice. However, if I were to see children dying during an epidemic, I could easily understand the rationale for mandating vaccines. I have already seen children die of tetanus in Africa and suffering from HiB meningitis in the United States. Whenever I think about someone in the intensive care unit with a vaccine-preventable disease, I am reminded of the rationale for vaccinations.

On February 12, 2009, after extensive review and deliberation of the available scientific evidence, three Special Masters of the U.S. Court of Federal Claims unanimously ruled that the MMR vaccine is not associated with autism or autism spectrum disorders. This is the first ruling in the Omnibus Autism Proceeding. The second ruling, which will evaluate whether there is any association between thimerosal and autism, is due later in 2009.

Chapter 5

HOW TO EVALUATE VACCINES

- What is a risk-benefit analysis?
- Why do you recommend a risk-benefit analysis for vaccines?
- What are some problems with a risk-benefit analysis?
- What is involved in a risk-benefit analysis for vaccines?
- What else should you consider in a vaccine risk-benefit analysis?
- How do I make the final decision about vaccines?
- What should I do if I decide that I don't want to vaccinate my child or that I want to choose an alternative vaccine schedule?
- What are some common alternative vaccine schedules?
- What would happen if we stopped vaccinations?
- What would happen if we stopped vaccinating against measles?
- What would happen if we stopped vaccinating against pertussis?
- What would happen if we stopped vaccinating against rubella (German measles)?
- What if we stopped vaccinating against diphtheria?
- What if we stopped vaccinating against Haemophilus influenzae type B (HiB)?

What is a risk-benefit analysis?

A risk-benefit analysis is a process where you consciously evaluate the various risks and benefits of a decision in order to make the best possible choice.

There are several important concepts in that definition. First, you are expected to "consciously" evaluate the risks and benefits. This means that you go beyond your gut instinct, your initial impression, and seek out additional information that might affect the decision. This additional information might be factual ("There is a one in one thousand risk of a stroke without this surgery"), but it also might be emotional ("I'm more scared of heart surgery than I am of a stroke").

The next concept involves the "various risks and benefits." These should be as broadly defined as you need. Any risk or any benefit that affects your personal decision is a valid one. For example, if you are buying a new car, you might feel that the risk of global warming is important enough to include in your risk-benefit analysis.

Finally, the goal is the "best" possible choice. "Best" is defined by you and doesn't have to be entirely rational. If you are particularly scared of planes, you might choose to drive across the country instead of flying, even though your risk of an accident is lower while flying.

Why do you recommend a risk-benefit analysis for vaccines?

I recommend performing a risk-benefit analysis for vaccines because I think that most people are already subconsciously evaluating vaccines in this manner. My goal is to make the process more explicit, more obvious, and more transparent. I think that by clearly outlining a thought process, people will come to more clarity in their decision-making process and therefore be more comfortable with their final decision.

For example, I regularly encounter parents who are concerned with certain vaccines or certain side effects and thus decline certain vaccines. In our discussion, I ask them to answer this question: If your family was traveling to a third-world country where you would be exposing your child to polio, measles, and other vaccine-preventable illnesses, would you consider vaccinating your child with these troublesome vaccines? Almost every parent answers yes.

Their answer shows that they are willing to consider individual vaccines on a case-by-case basis. In this example, they are declining vaccinations in the United States, where there is a low risk of contracting these diseases, because they feel that the vaccine's benefits do not outweigh the risks. However, when traveling to a country where the risk of getting the illness is higher, they are deciding that the benefits of the vaccines outweigh the risk of any side effects. They are weighing the risks of the vaccine (known and unknown side effects) versus the benefits of the vaccine (minimized risk of contracting the disease). They are already doing their own risk-benefit analysis.

In the end, this type of analysis helps you identify what factors you want to consider when deciding about certain vaccines. It also demonstrates to hesitant parents that under certain circumstances, they might decide to vaccinate their child.

What are some problems with a risk-benefit analysis?

Unfortunately, this kind of risk-benefit analysis is not easy to do and is riddled with problems. From a statistical point of view, people are not very good about assessing risk. For example, most people are far more afraid of flying on a plane than driving on a highway, even though the actual risk of injury or death is much higher when driving. We tend to underestimate risks when we feel we are in control (we are driving) and overestimate them when someone else is in control (the pilot is flying the plane). Similarly, when some parents decide not to vaccinate, they feel in control and may underestimate the risks. Because the vaccines are manufactured and given by others, these parents may feel less in control and may overestimate the risks.

We also have a hard time comprehending small risks. We can generally grasp a one in ten risk, maybe even a one in a hundred risk. However, once the risk is higher, people tend to lump them all in a category of "low risk," not distinguishing between a one in a thousand and a one in a million risk. Those risks are markedly different, though. If four million babies are born every year in the United States, a one in a thousand risk affects four thousand babies where a one in a million risk affects only four babies. The risks associated with vaccines and with the diseases they prevent are often in the range of one in a thousand to one in a million. So when we lump these "low risk" events together, we might not realize that some events are truly riskier than others and that more children might be affected.

It is also hard to separate out the emotional overlay in a risk-benefit analysis. In my opinion, you shouldn't try to remove emotions from the decision, but you should try to recognize hidden emotions. By opening them up to the light of day, you might begin to see how they are influencing your decision.

You can then decide if you want to give them that much influence.

For example, I have a family in my practice that had a child born with a specific genetic abnormality. The diagnosis was very unexpected because their prenatal testing had put them at low risk for this problem— around one in five hundred pregnancies. The situation was very hard on the parents, and it took time for them to adjust to their child's special needs.

When they became pregnant again, they were clear they did not want to risk facing this genetic abnormality again. They opted for every prenatal test, no matter how low the risk of abnormality. They knew they were not making decisions based on statistics but on emotions. In this risk-benefit analysis, their emotions were the driving factors.

What is involved in a risk-benefit analysis for vaccines?

The rational decision-making portion of a risk-benefit analysis for vaccines is fairly straightforward. For simplicity's sake, you can break down each vaccine into two choices: to give or not to give the vaccine. In reality there are other options such as giving the vaccine on a different schedule or breaking combination vaccines into separate components. If you wanted to include those possibilities, you could represent those options as additional choices in your analysis. For simplicity's sake, I will just consider the "to give or not to give" options in this discussion.

You then need to ask about the risks and benefits of each decision. For example, if you give the vaccine, you have the risk of side effects. You then need to know how often each side effect occurs and how mild or serious the complications of these side effects are. You will probably have less concern for a two-day fever than for a hospitalization for encephalitis. You also need to know how effective the vaccine is so you can calculate the amount of protection or other benefits you might derive from it.

On the other hand, if you don't give the vaccine, you have the risk of the disease itself. You need to know how common the disease is and how likely you or your child is to be exposed. You also need to know the consequences of the disease, both mild and severe, and how likely those consequences are. Are we talking about a one in a thousand risk or a one in a million?

In the end, you hopefully will be able to judge the relative risk of the vaccine compared to the risk of the disease from *your* perspective. I have spent most of parts II, III, and IV of this book providing these factual details for the most common vaccines available in the United States.

What else should you consider in a vaccine risk-benefit analysis?

The first part of the risk-benefit analysis previously described is more rational, more mathematical, and more logical. You should also factor in some less-rational issues in your decision-making process.

First, you need to think about how you view public health versus your individual child's health. As described in chapter 2, the public health viewpoint is that the benefits of vaccinating everyone outweigh the side effects, even the serious side effects, that some children suffer from the vaccines. In short, the benefits for the many outweigh the harm to the few. For most parents, this is generally true, unless the harm is to their child. So how much are you willing to support public health if it increases the risk to your own child?

Now, if you don't vaccinate, you might be counting on herd immunity to last so you can avoid the risk to your own child from both the disease *and* the vaccine. But you also have to ask yourself what would happen if lots of people stopped vaccinating. If enough people stop vaccinating, then herd immunity will fail, and your child will be at a higher risk from the disease because it is more common. So how do you factor in the increased risk to your child as a member of the local population if herd immunity fails?

You also need to consider your belief system with regards to medicine. I have a few parents who don't trust doctors, who don't trust the government, and who don't trust corporations. They obviously have a very difficult time trusting anything I say about vaccines.

There are also families who don't believe in medical treatments but feel that alternative therapies are better able to protect their children from disease. They believe in acupuncture and organic foods and homeopathy. They feel that vaccines are unnatural and harmful to the body and that contracting the disease is the most natural way to build immunity. They too have their own hesitations about vaccines.

Again, that is not to say that my opinion is right and their opinion is wrong. I am merely pointing out that these beliefs should be clearly on the table and recognized as key influences on the final decision.

How do I make the final decision about vaccines?

After you analyze all the rational and emotional influences regarding vaccines, you need to realize that you have to make a decision that you can live with for the rest of your life. You are going to feel terrible if you decide to vaccinate and your child has some terrible side effect that harms him or her for life. But you are also going to feel terrible if you don't vaccinate and your child gets the illness the vaccine could have prevented and has some rare consequence that also harms him or her for life.

As I have said many times, I personally and professionally believe that the benefits of vaccines outweigh the risks associated with vaccines, and I recommend to all my patients that they receive the vaccines on schedule. However, in the end, I am not the person who has to live with the decision. You are. So gather as much information as possible, either from this book or other sources, and make the best decision you can for yourself and your family.

What should I do if I decide that I don't want to vaccinate my child or that I want to choose an alternative vaccine schedule?

First, you should research your state and local laws regarding vaccinations. This will be helpful if you ever decide to enroll your child in day care or public school. You need to know what kind of vaccine exemptions are allowed (medical, religious, and/or personal or philosophical) and which vaccines are required in your school district. Some vaccines that are recommended by the CDC are not required in some states for entry into school or day care.

The next thing to do is to discuss the matter with your doctor. Unfortunately, some physicians feel so uncomfortable with a parent's decision to not vaccinate that they ask the family to leave the practice. The American Academy of Pediatrics does not agree with that position. The *2006 Report of the Committee on Infectious Diseases* states that in general, physicians "should avoid discharging a patient from their practice solely because a parent refuses immunizations for the child." However, if you have a physician who feels strongly enough about vaccines to discharge you from the practice if you decide not to vaccinate, then that physician will probably not be a good fit for your family, and you should probably find a new doctor.

If you are able to have a comfortable discussion with your doctor, explain your thinking, and then listen to the doctor's response. He or she might be able to correct some misinformation that you have heard and guide you to respected sources of information. Your doctor might be able to point out the flaws on the website that you have been reading. Or your doctor might agree that there are certain rare but real risks to a certain vaccine and empathize with your difficult decision.

For most physicians, this type of conversation about vaccines might best be approached outside the context of a well-child checkup. It requires more time than is usually allotted for a regular checkup, so you may need to make an extra appointment to have a lengthy discussion about vaccines. Alternatively, you might ask for extra time at the two-month well-child checkup. In my practice, I bring up the issue of vaccines at the two- to three-week well-child checkup to get a sense of the parents' feelings about vaccines. If I notice some hesitation, I refer them to several sources about vaccines and also make sure my staff schedules extra time at the two-month well-child checkup.

In the end, you should come up with a vaccine schedule that works for you and your family. Even though it might mean more work for his or her office, your doctor should consent to your request for an alternative schedule.

And if you flat-out refuse to administer any vaccines to your child, make sure that doesn't sour your relationship with your doctor. In my office, I try not to take it personally and repeat my mantra: My job is to give parents information; their job is to decide what to do with that information. However, I ask that they politely listen to me at every well-child checkup as I recommend the vaccines. If they then decide to not vaccinate, that is their decision.

You can review more information about vaccine exemptions at the end of chapter 4.

What are some common alternative vaccine schedules?

The most common alternative vaccine schedule that I have encountered involves merely spreading the vaccines out over time. Instead of giving eight vaccines (involving at least three injections and one oral vaccine) at the two-, four-, and six-month well-child checkups, parents choose to give fewer vaccines at the checkups and then come back later for the remaining vaccines.

Some parents choose to return in between the well-child checkups for the additional vaccines. This allows them to be caught up by seven months of age. I discussed the most extreme example of this pattern in chapter 4, where the mother insisted on giving each vaccine separately and came back every week for several weeks in a row, starting the whole cycle over again at the next checkup. Other parents spread the vaccines out over a longer period of time, with the goal of being caught up by age two.

Another common alternative vaccine schedule I have seen parents choose focuses on giving certain, more critical, vaccines to infants and delaying less critical vaccines until the child is older. Under this schedule, parents focus on the HiB, pediatric pneumococcal, and DTaP vaccines, as they protect against diseases that are particularly dangerous for young babies. However, the parents often choose to delay the polio and hepatitis B vaccines until the child is much older because the risk of contracting those diseases is so low.

Another alternative vaccine schedule that has become more common in my practice is the one recommended in *The Vaccine Book* by Dr. Robert Sears. He generally recommends not giving more than two vaccines at the same time. In addition, he focuses on the aluminum content of certain vaccines when choosing which two vaccines should be given at any one visit.

Please remember that none of these alternative schedules has been tested in studies. They are all based on assumptions that have not been proven true or false. If it gives you more comfort to choose an alternative schedule and your child ultimately ends up completely vaccinated, that is your choice, and I will support your decision. However, if you don't have a strong feeling in favor of an alternative schedule, I always suggest following the recommended vaccine schedule.

What would happen if we stopped vaccinations?

There are two ways of viewing a world without vaccinations. First, you can review data from before the vaccine era to see how many cases of a certain disease occurred and how serious the most severe cases were. Alternatively, you can review examples of recent epidemics where herd immunity was not sufficient and people contracted certain diseases. I will use both types of data in the following paragraphs.

What would happen if we stopped vaccinating against measles?

Measles is one of the most contagious diseases known. Over 90 percent of unimmunized people who are exposed to the measles virus will develop the disease. Before the vaccine era, measles was considered a rite of passage in childhood, with millions of cases in the United States every year. Of those millions of cases, thousands of people were admitted to the hospital due to complications, and an average of 450 people died every year in the 1950s.

More recently, there was a measles epidemic in the United States from 1989 to 1991, affecting fifty-five thousand people. This epidemic occurred during an era when the United States had high-quality sanitation and excellent medical facilities, and there were still 132 deaths from complications related to measles. Since then, the recommendation has been to give two doses of measles vaccine to all children before they enter kindergarten.

If you think this epidemic is an anomaly, Japan repealed mandatory immunization laws in the 1990s and suffered an epidemic of two hundred thousand cases of measles in 2000, with almost a hundred deaths. Another outbreak involving hundreds of students occurred in Tokyo in 2007.

Finally, in 2008, the rate of measles cases in the United States almost quadrupled, going from an average of 63 a year to 131 cases in the first seven months of 2008. Almost every case could be linked to an imported case of measles. However, the significant rise in number of cases did not occur because of more imported cases but rather because the same number of imported cases spread more widely among unvaccinated children. Although the numbers were small, this is an example of how herd immunity can fail with a highly contagious disease.

What would happen if we stopped vaccinating against pertussis?

Pertussis, or whooping cough, is still present in the United States. I just received laboratory confirmation of the diagnosis yesterday in a five-year-old child and have had two other cases in the last month. My small town of fifty thousand has had an epidemic of around a hundred cases every other year since 2000. Nationally, there were over twenty-five thousand cases in the United States in 2004.

So if we stopped vaccinating against pertussis, there would be a huge increase in the number of cases of whooping cough. This would be most dangerous for newborns and young infants, who have the highest rate of hospitalization, pneumonia, seizures, coma, and death. In the prevaccine era, around two hundred thousand pertussis cases were reported annually in the United States, with over nine thousand deaths.

This increase in cases of pertussis has been seen in various other countries where the use of the pertussis vaccine has declined. In both Japan and the United Kingdom, the vaccination rate against pertussis declined in the 1970s because parents were hesitant to vaccinate. Both countries suffered epidemics with thousands of cases and thirty to forty deaths. A well-respected study published in *The Lancet* medical journal in 1998 showed that in countries with lower immunization rates, there was a ten to one hundred times increase in the rate of pertussis when compared to countries with higher immunization rates.

What would happen if we stopped vaccinating against rubella (German measles)?

The major goal of the rubella vaccine is not to protect the recipient from German measles. The illness is very mild, slightly worse than the common cold, with only rare side effects. However, if a pregnant mother develops rubella, she is at increased risk of having a miscarriage. In addition, her baby is at increased risk of congenital rubella syndrome, which includes blindness, deafness, or mental retardation, and an increased risk of death.

Before the rubella vaccine was developed, there were regular epidemics of rubella in the United States. One epidemic from 1964 to 1965 led to an estimated eleven thousand miscarriages, two thousand infant deaths, and over twenty thousand infants born with congenital rubella syndrome. By comparison, in

2000, only six cases of congenital rubella syndrome were reported, mostly from immigrants who did not receive the vaccine in their country of birth. So if we stopped vaccinating against rubella, we would see a large increase in the number of birth defects due to congenital rubella syndrome as well as a large increase in the number of miscarriages.

What if we stopped vaccinating against diphtheria?

This experiment has already occurred in the former Soviet Union. In the turmoil of the early 1990s, the public health system failed to continue its mass vaccination program. Subsequently, the newly independent countries experienced an epidemic of diphtheria. While most modern countries have a rate of less than ten cases a year, these countries had an average of fifteen thousand cases a year in the 1990s, with an average of five hundred deaths annually. So if we stopped vaccinating against diphtheria, we too might experience such an epidemic.

What if we stopped vaccinating against Haemophilus influenzae type B (HiB)?

The HiB vaccine is near and dear to my heart. While I have seen mild cases of whooping cough, I have never had to have a child admitted to the hospital because of pertussis. I have also never seen a case of measles, rubella or congenital rubella syndrome, or diphtheria. But I am old enough to have seen a case of HiB meningitis, and I still remember how sick that little baby was when I admitted him to the hospital.

In 1985 there were approximately twenty thousand cases of severe HiB disease in the United States, with the majority of those infections causing meningitis. In 1995 there were less than a hundred cases of severe HiB disease. The HiB vaccine came out in the late 1980s and effectively wiped out HiB meningitis and other severe HiB infections.

So if we stopped vaccinating against HiB, we would return to the days of my medical training, and we would see this deadly disease again. I, for one, never want to have to take care of another child with HiB meningitis.

Part II
Vaccines in the First Year of Life

The next several chapters focus on specific vaccines either recommended for all children and/or adults or recommended in certain circumstances. Remember, if you don't have any concerns about vaccines, I recommend all the vaccines listed. I feel that the benefits outweigh the risks, both for the individual and for society as a whole.

However, knowing that many people have concerns about some or all vaccines, I will carefully analyze each vaccine using the following questions:

- What is disease X and what kind of problems does it cause?
- How serious and how treatable is the disease X infection?
- How is disease X transmitted and how likely is my child to get disease X?
- What kind of vaccine for disease X exists and when is it usually given?

- How effective is the disease X vaccine?
- How serious and how common are the side effects of the disease X vaccine?
- What are the medical reasons to not give the disease X vaccine?
- What is Dr. Jamie's overall recommendation for the disease X vaccine?

These questions allow you to evaluate the risks and benefits of each vaccine and hopefully make you more comfortable with your final decision.

Chapter 6

THE PNEUMOCOCCAL VACCINE FOR YOUNG CHILDREN

- What is pneumococcus and what kind of problems does it cause?
- How serious and how treatable is a pneumococcal infection?
- How is pneumococcus transmitted and how likely is my child to get pneumococcus?
- What kind of vaccines for pneumococcus exist and when are they usually given?
- How effective is the pneumococcal vaccine?
- How serious and how common are the side effects of the pneumococcal vaccine?
- What are the medical reasons to not give the pneumo-coccal vaccine?
- What is Dr. Jamie's overall recommendation for the pneumococcal vaccine?

What is pneumococcus and what kind of problems does it cause?

Pneumococcus (plural pneumococci) is another name for the *Streptococcus pneumoniae* bacterium. These bacteria are related to group A streptococcus (which cause strep throat) but were commonly found in the lungs and given the name pneumoniae. Pneumococcus can infect many parts of the body, not just the lungs, causing meningitis, sepsis (infection of the blood-stream), ear infections, and joint infections.

How serious and how treatable is a pneumococcal infection?

Pneumococcal infections can range from mild to severe. There are an estimated five million pneumococcal ear infections each year in the United States, plus over ten thousand bloodstream infections and several hundred cases of meningitis. Over two hundred children a year die from complications of these infections, and many other children are left with lifelong consequences, such as brain damage and hearing loss. Thus, these can be very serious infections.

The majority of the milder infections are easily treated with oral antibiotics at home. The more serious infections require intravenous (IV) antibiotics in the hospital and occasionally require spinal taps. Unfortunately, some of the bacteria have become resistant to common antibiotics such as penicillin, which makes them harder to treat.

How is pneumococcus transmitted and how likely is my child to get pneumococcus?

Pneumococci are transmitted by respiratory droplets (coughs and sneezes) and by direct contact with a person's oral secretions (through sharing toys, cups, spoons, etc.). Commonsense hand-washing techniques can decrease the risk of transmitting or receiving the infection.

Unfortunately, pneumococci are common in the United States. There are thousands of severe infections in children and millions of milder infections as well. In addition, there are tens of thousands of severe infections in adults. Thus, it is extremely likely that your child will be exposed to this disease. In fact, there are several subtypes, called serotypes, of the bacteria, so your child will likely be repeatedly exposed.

What kinds of vaccines for pneumococcus exist and when are they usually given?

There are two vaccines for pneumococcal disease, one with seven serotypes (PCV7) and one with twenty-three serotypes (PPV23). Both vaccines are polysaccharide vaccines. This means that because only part of the bacteria was used to make the vaccine, it is impossible to develop the disease from the vaccine.

PCV7 has the brand name of Prevnar and is recommended for children up to age five. The routine schedule recommends a dose at two, four, and six months, with a booster at twelve to fifteen months.

PPV23 has the brand name of Pneumovax and is recommended for anyone over sixty-five and for younger adults with certain diseases, such as diabetes. In the fall of 2008, the recommendation for Pneumovax was extended to all smokers and anyone with asthma. In certain high-risk children, Pneumovax can be given as early as age two, with one repeat dose three to five years later.

How effective is the pneumococcal vaccine?

In general, both vaccines are very effective. Prevnar is the more recent introduction into the vaccine schedule (starting in 2000), and research is ongoing. However, it appears that invasive illness from the seven serotypes included in the vaccine has decreased significantly. Pneumovax has been around for decades and is very effective in the elderly. The major drawback with both vaccines is that they only cover some of the more than ninety existing serotypes. While the serotypes included in each vaccine were chosen because they were the most likely to cause infections, there are dozens remaining for which we do not have a vaccine.

How serious and how common are the side effects of the pneumococcal vaccine?

The Prevnar vaccine has had no serious or permanent side effects noted. However, there is a significant risk of a fever and a slight risk (2 percent) of a high fever over 102°F. My own daughter suffered from this side effect and despite my reassurances, my wife stopped giving her this vaccine after two doses when each dose was followed by a fever of 103°F. There is also a one in four chance of a mild side effect such as redness, tenderness, or swelling at the injection site.

The Pneumovax is a very safe vaccine, with less than 1 percent of recipients developing anything more than a sore arm. Unfortunately, despite its safety, it is not effective in children under age two and thus cannot be used in infants.

What are the medical reasons to not give the pneumococcal vaccine?

The pneumococcal vaccine should not be given to anyone who has had a severe allergic reaction to a previous dose of the vaccine or to any component in the vaccine. In addition, people who are moderately or severely ill should be cautioned against receiving this vaccine until they recover from their illness. The PPV23 vaccine (Pneumovax) has not been studied in pregnant women, but there is no evidence or theoretical belief that it would be harmful for the mother or the fetus.

What is Dr. Jamie's overall recommendation for the pneumococcal vaccine?

This is one of my top two vaccine recommendations. Pneumococcus is a very common illness in the United States, with the potential of serious consequences. The side effects are usually mild and even when the high fever occurs, it goes away without any permanent effects. I strongly recommend this vaccine.

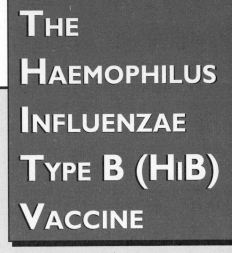

Chapter 7

THE HAEMOPHILUS INFLUENZAE TYPE B (HIB) VACCINE

- What is HiB and what kind of problems does it cause?
- How serious and how treatable is the HiB infection?
- How is HiB transmitted and how likely is my child to get HiB?
- What kind of vaccine for HiB exists and when is it usually given?
- How effective is the HiB vaccine?
- How serious and how common are the side effects of the HiB vaccine?
- What are the medical reasons to not give the HiB vaccine?
- What is Dr. Jamie's overall recommendation for the HiB vaccine?

What is HiB and what kind of problems does it cause?

HiB is one of many strains of the Haemophilus influenzae bacteria and is identified by a particular type of sugar on its cell wall. HiB frequently resides in the mouth and nose without causing a problem. This is called the asymptomatic carrier state and can occur from only 4 percent of the time in the community to over 40 percent of the time in hospital day cares. Thus, it is very common to be exposed to HiB in the course of daily activities.

However, occasionally HiB will invade other parts of the body and cause a variety of infections, including meningitis (an infection of the brain and spinal cord), epiglottis (an infection and swelling of the covering of the esophagus, which can lead to blockage of the breathing passages), and pneumonia.

How serious and how treatable is the HiB infection?

HiB is a serious infection in children under the age of five. Even in the best case scenario, treatment requires hospitalization for more than a week with IV antibiotics. If meningitis is involved, repeated lumbar punctures (spinal taps) are required. If epiglottis is involved, the child might need to be intubated (have a breathing tube placed down his or her throat). Most children survive, but about 5 percent die, even with the best possible care. Between 20 and 40 percent of affected children suffer long-term consequences, such as hearing impairment or residual brain damage.

There is an antibiotic called Rifampin that is available if someone in your family is exposed to a confirmed case of HiB. Rifampin is given to the entire family to try to clear HiB from the nose and mouth. It is only needed for families with young children who are incompletely vaccinated against HiB.

How is HiB transmitted and how likely is my child to get HiB?

HiB is transmitted by coughing or by direct contact with another child's mucus or saliva. The latter situation might occur by a child sharing toys or eating utensils. The common precautions of washing your child's hands frequently and staying several feet away from coughing children will help decrease the spread of HiB.

Currently, thanks to the vaccine, your child is unlikely to get HiB in the United States. There are now fewer than a hundred cases of invasive HiB per year in the United States. In addition, the vaccine has also decreased the asymptomatic carrier state. This makes it unlikely that your child will get the bacteria from another child who is carrying the bacteria but is not sick.

What kind of vaccine for HiB exists and when is it usually given?

There are currently two brands of the HiB vaccine available in the United States: ActHIB and PedVaxHIB. (A third brand of the HiB vaccine, HibTITER, was discontinued in 2007.) Both of the available brands are polysaccharide conjugate vaccines and are given intramuscularly by an injection. (Remember that it is not possible to contract the disease from a polysaccharide vaccine.) The recommended schedule for ActHIB is to give the vaccine at two, four, and six months, plus another booster at twelve to fifteen months. The PedVaxHIB brand has a similar schedule, except that it does not require a dose at six months. There is a catch-up schedule available if your child starts the sequence late and missed some of the earlier doses.

Although the HiB vaccine is not usually given after age five, in certain circumstances, the HiB vaccine is recommended for older children and adults. These special circumstances include sickle cell disease, removal of the spleen, or certain cancer treatments.

How effective is the HiB vaccine?

The HiB vaccine is very effective. Since the vaccine became universally recommended in the United States, the incidence of HiB has decreased by over 99 percent. Before the vaccine became widely available in the 1980s, there were about twenty thousand cases of invasive HiB annually in the United States in children younger than five years old. Now there are less than a hundred.

How serious and how common are the side effects of the HiB vaccine?

The side effects of the HiB vaccine are very mild and not very common. About 5 percent of children will have a low-grade fever up to 101°F. Up to 25 percent of children will have redness, warmth, or swelling at the injection site. There have been no moderate or severe side effects noted for this vaccine at all. There was a concern in an Australian study that linked the HiB vaccine to an increased risk for juvenile diabetes, but additional research has failed to confirm that concern.

What are the medical reasons to not give the HiB vaccine?

The HiB vaccine should not be given to anyone who has had a severe allergic reaction to a previous dose of the vaccine or to any component in the vaccine. In addition, people who are moderately or severely ill should be cautioned against receiving this vaccine until they recover from their illness. Otherwise, there are no medical reasons to not receive the vaccine. The HiB vaccine is only approved for individuals over the age of six weeks.

What is Dr. Jamie's overall recommendation for the HiB vaccine?

The HiB vaccine is one of my top two vaccine recommendations, especially for nervous parents who are hesitant about vaccines. The common side effects are mild, and the lack of any severe side effects is very reassuring. In addition, the disease, although rare, is severe when it occurs. Finally, the vaccine is extremely effective, with a dramatic decrease in the presence of the disease in just ten years. I strongly recommend this vaccine.

Chapter 8

THE DIPHTHERIA, TETANUS, AND ACELLULAR PERTUSSIS (DTaP) VACCINE

- ■ What are diphtheria, tetanus, and pertussis and what kind of problems do they cause?
- ■ How serious and how treatable are diphtheria, tetanus, and pertussis infections?
- ■ How are diphtheria, tetanus, and pertussis transmitted and how likely is my child to get one of these infections?
- ■ What kind of vaccine for diphtheria, tetanus, and pertussis exists and when is it usually given?
- ■ How effective is the diphtheria, tetanus, and pertussis vaccine?
- ■ How serious and how common are the side effects of the diphtheria, tetanus, and pertussis vaccine?
- ■ What are the medical reasons to not give any of the tetanus-, diphtheria-, or pertussis-containing vaccines?
- ■ What is Dr. Jamie's overall recommendation for the diphtheria, tetanus, and pertussis vaccine?

What are diphtheria, tetanus, and pertussis and what kind of problems do they cause?

Diphtheria is a bacterial infection that infects the throat and nose and can form a membrane that restricts the flow of air into the lungs.

Tetanus is a bacterial infection that is introduced into the body via a deep and dirty cut in the skin. As the bacteria grow, they produce a toxin that affects the nerves, blocking certain signals to the muscles. This leads to muscle spasms, including those of the jaw. This is where the common name for tetanus, "lockjaw," originated.

Pertussis, or whooping cough, is a bacterial respiratory infection associated with a severe cough. The coughs are often batched together and can last for over thirty seconds. By the end of the batch of coughs, the infected person gasps for breath and makes a characteristic "whoop" in order to get oxygen into his or her lungs. In infants, the whoop might be missing, but the baby temporarily stops breathing for several seconds.

How serious and how treatable are diphtheria, tetanus, and pertussis infections?

These infections are very serious. Even with high-quality medical care, over 3 percent of cases of diphtheria are fatal. Occasionally the membrane obstructs the airway, requiring intubation (placement of a tube down the throat to allow air to pass). In addition, the bacteria's toxin can affect the heart and some nerves. Treatment includes both antibiotics and a special treatment using horse antitoxin.

Tetanus can be serious if untreated. The World Health Organization estimated that over 180,000 newborns died of neonatal tetanus in 2002. These deaths occurred because of poor hygiene at the delivery. In addition, the lack of tetanus vaccinations for the mother meant that she had no protective antibodies to pass to her newborn baby.

However, in the United States, tetanus is very treatable. Tetanus immune globulin (an injection of antibodies that will directly attack the bacteria), antibiotics, and appropriate wound care are the mainstay of treatment. Specific medications are also helpful in controlling the pain of muscle spasms.

Pertussis is most severe in infants younger than six months old. About 1 percent of hospitalized children die, and up to 20 percent have pneumonia, seizures, or brain damage. Treatment for these children requires antibiotics and supportive care, such as managing their oxygen, fluids, and nutrition while they are trying to breathe. Sometimes ICU care is required.

Older children and adults have milder cases of pertussis. They might have lingering coughs for weeks to months but usually only require oral antibiotics at home.

How are diphtheria, tetanus, and pertussis transmitted and how likely is my child to get one of these infections?

The bacteria for diphtheria are present in the eye, nose, and throat discharge of an infected person and are spread by close contact with another person. It is very unlikely that your child will ever be exposed to this disease because there is now only an average of five cases per year in the United States.

Tetanus is unique because it is the only vaccine-preventable illness that cannot be spread from person to person. The bacteria are found in the soil and are spread to humans when dirt enters a break in the skin. Thus, the likelihood of contracting tetanus is entirely related to the number of dirty wounds your child experiences and how those wounds are managed. Appropriate care of wounds with extensive washing is important in preventing your child's exposure to tetanus.

While tetanus is not common in the United States, it is a significant cause of death internationally.

Worldwide, tens of thousands of infants die every year from neonatal tetanus. I still have vivid memories of seeing newborn children die from tetanus when I was practicing in Africa during my training. These infections could be prevented by immunizing pregnant women. After the mothers developed appropriate antibodies, they would pass them on to their children as part of the maternal transfer of antibodies that occurs late in pregnancy. If the babies had some antibodies at birth, they might be better able to fight off neonatal tetanus.

Pertussis is spread by droplets from coughing. Unfortunately, it is easy to spread the infection. First, infected individuals are contagious for two to six weeks. Second, the infection starts out mildly and does not seem serious at first, so the antibiotics that would stop the spread of the infection are delayed. Some research suggests that up to 80 percent of unimmunized household members will develop the disease.

As for your particular child, it depends on how common pertussis is in your community. Epidemics occur every two to five years in many communities. This is probably because the immunity wanes in adolescents and adults and they can be reinfected, starting the infection cycle all over again.

What kind of vaccine for diphtheria, tetanus, and pertussis exists and when is it usually given?

The most common vaccine for these three diseases is a combination vaccine for diphtheria, tetanus, and acellular pertussis, abbreviated as DTaP. The acellular pertussis is a less reactive version of the pertussis vaccine than the whole-cell pertussis DTP vaccine that was used before the mid-1990s. This decreased reactivity makes the DTaP vaccine safer than the old DTP vaccine. This vaccine is scheduled to be given at two, four, and six months, with another booster at fifteen to eighteen months and a final booster at four to six years.

A new variation of this vaccine is Tdap. This vaccine is recommended for adolescents and adults in order to boost their immunity to pertussis. The tetanus (T) component of the vaccine is the same as DTaP, but the diphtheria (d) and acellular pertussis (ap) have less diphtheria toxoid and less pertussis antigen than in DTaP. The schedule for this vaccine for children is once at age eleven or twelve.

Adults are recommended to substitute Tdap for their next tetanus booster vaccine and then continue with the regular tetanus boosters for the rest of their lives. Healthcare workers and any new parent or infant caretakers, especially of infants less than twelve months old, are recommended to get Tdap as soon as possible, even if they received a tetanus booster recently. This recommendation is aimed at preventing the spread of pertussis to infants who are more likely to have a severe case.

The value of the Tdap recommendation for healthcare workers was driven home to me by a CDC report published in June 2008. It reported on a healthcare worker in Texas who unknowingly spread pertussis to eleven infants on a maternity ward. She had been appropriately vaccinated as a child but had not received the Tdap vaccination because it was not yet available in 2004. During the investigation, she was the only healthcare worker who tested positive for pertussis. Of the eleven infants, four were admitted to the pediatric intensive care unit, and five others were admitted to the general pediatric hospital. Fortunately, none of the affected infants died.

There are two brands of the Tdap vaccine: Adacel and Boostrix. The Adacel vaccine is approved for people ages eleven to sixty-four years. The Boostrix vaccine was originally approved for ages ten to eighteen years but received an expanded approval in December 2008 that extended its use to include ages ten to sixty-four years.

Other variations of this vaccine include the DT and Td vaccines. The DT vaccine is suggested for children younger than seven years of age when the pertussis vaccine is not recommended. It provides the pediatric dose of diphtheria and tetanus without any pertussis. It can be used in place of DTaP at any point in the schedule that the DTaP vaccine is recommended. The Td vaccine is the adolescent and adult booster for tetanus and diphtheria and is recommended for people seven years of age and older. It should be given once every ten years (unless Tdap is preferred).

Finally, there is a tetanus-only version of the vaccine for when both diphtheria and pertussis are not recommended. This is only approved for individuals seven years of age and older.

All of these vaccines are inactivated, or killed, vaccines.

How effective is the diphtheria, tetanus, and pertussis vaccine?

These vaccines are apparently very effective; they clearly induce protective antibodies in individuals who receive them. Other evidence of effectiveness is more circumstantial. There are currently less than five cases of diphtheria and less than fifty cases of tetanus in the United States every year, compared to thousands or hundreds of thousands in other parts of the world. Some of this might be related to better medical care and sanitation, but not all. One important point is that the effectiveness of the pertussis vaccine wanes over time. This is why we now recommend the Tdap vaccine, which is a pertussis booster, for adolescents and adults.

How serious and how common are the side effects of the diphtheria, tetanus, and pertussis vaccine?

This is the major issue with this vaccine. While the Td and DT vaccines rarely cause more than a sore arm, the Tdap and DTaP vaccines have many more side effects. The additional side effects are presumably from the pertussis component of the vaccines.

For the DTaP vaccine, the Vaccine Information Statement (VIS) has a long list of possible side effects. These start with mild reactions: fever, redness, swelling, tenderness, and others in up to one in three recipients. The next level of reactions are called "moderate": nonstop crying for more than three hours in one child in a thousand, seizures in one child in fourteen thousand, high fever over 105°F in one child in sixteen thousand. The final level of reactions is classified as "severe": a severe allergic reaction, long-term seizures, coma, lowered consciousness, and permanent brain damage. While the severe allergic reaction is listed as occurring in less than one out of a million doses, the other severe reactions are listed as so rare that experts are not sure if they are caused by the vaccine. However, the moderate reactions are real and scary enough.

The Tdap vaccine has fewer side effects listed, and most of them are similar to the mild reactions previously covered: pain, redness, fever, plus some nausea, vomiting, and headaches. None were reported as permanent but interestingly enough, they occurred more often than with the DTaP vaccine, in up to 75 percent of the recipients in some cases.

What are the medical reasons to not give any of the tetanus-, diphtheria-, or pertussis-containing vaccines?

These vaccines should not be given to anyone who has had a severe allergic reaction to a previous dose of the vaccine or to any component in the vaccine. In addition, people who are moderately or severely ill should be cautioned against receiving this vaccine until they recover from their illness.

Children who had encephalopathy or a coma within seven days of a previous DTaP vaccine should never receive another DTaP or Tdap vaccine. In addition, children who have a progressive or unstable neurological condition, such as uncontrolled seizures, or progressive encephalopathy, should not receive the vaccine until their neurological status has stabilized. Children who have a stable neurological condition, such as cerebral palsy, should receive the vaccine.

Children who had a moderate or severe reaction to a previous dose of DTaP should discuss the option of using the DT vaccine without a pertussis component for subsequent vaccines in the series. Such reactions might include shock or collapse, a seizure, a fever greater than or equal to 105°F, or nonstop crying for more than three hours after a previous dose of DTaP.

People considering the Tdap vaccine should talk to their doctor if they have ever had Guillain-Barré syndrome (GBS) in the past.

The DTaP and DT vaccines are only approved for children under the age of seven years. The Td and tetanus alone vaccines are only recommended for people seven years of age and older. The two types of Tdap vaccine are approved for different ages, but together they cover a range of people aged ten to sixty-five years.

What is Dr. Jamie's overall recommendation for the diphtheria, tetanus, and pertussis vaccine?

The DTaP vaccine gets a reserved recommendation. The diseases are real and dangerous, and, in the case of pertussis, very common. In addition, the worst cases of pertussis occur in the youngest infants, which is why we recommend the vaccine starting at the age of two months. Overall, I recommend this vaccine, and it is actually my third choice for children, mainly because of the widespread nature of pertussis in the United States. However, the side effects are real and are not trivial. I completely understand why parents are hesitant to vaccinate with this vaccine.

If parents of young children decline to vaccinate with DTaP, I then recommend the DT vaccine for children under the age of seven. This provides the necessary protection from diphtheria and tetanus without the side effects of the acellular pertussis portion of the vaccine. As already mentioned, the pertussis component is responsible for the majority of the worrisome side effects of the DTaP vaccine, whereas the DT vaccine has minimal side effects. Unfortunately, you also lose the protection from pertussis, which is the more common and potentially more dangerous disease.

The case for Tdap is clearer. Pertussis is a common but mild disease in adolescents and adults. However, they are the people who spread it to infants, who then develop the severe disease. If we were able to vaccinate enough people to short-circuit the transmission of the bacteria (remember herd immunity on page 29?), we could prevent the hospitalizations and deaths in our youngest children. A single booster dose of Tdap could break the cycle. And even though there are many side effects with this vaccine, they are generally mild and never permanent. Thus, I recommend the Tdap vaccine.

I also recommend the Td vaccine. Everyone needs a booster to get protection from diphtheria and tetanus on a regular basis, and the Td vaccine every ten years fits the bill. However, some insurance plans don't pay for preventative vaccines but will pay for a Td vaccine after an injury. If you have received the primary series of three vaccines, it is unlikely that you will get a significant infection, no matter how deep the wound. And diphtheria is rare in the United States. So if you prefer to wait until you get a significant cut before getting your booster dose so that insurance will pay for the vaccine, that is an acceptable alternative.

Chapter 9

THE ROTAVIRUS VACCINE

- What is rotavirus and what kind of problems does it cause?
- How serious and how treatable is the rotavirus infection?
- How is rotavirus transmitted and how likely is my child to get rotavirus?
- What kind of vaccine for rotavirus exists and when is it usually given?
- How effective is the rotavirus vaccine?
- How serious and how common are the side effects of the rotavirus vaccine?
- What are the medical reasons to not give the rotavirus vaccine?
- What is Dr. Jamie's overall recommendation for the rotavirus vaccine?

What is rotavirus and what kind of problems does it cause?

Rotavirus is an intestinal, or stomach, virus that causes diarrhea. Because the diarrhea is more copious and frequent than with other viruses, it is easier for children to become dehydrated.

How serious and how treatable is the rotavirus infection?

In the United States, rotavirus can be serious but is rarely life threatening. Over fifty thousand children are admitted to the hospital each year due to rotavirus, and many more visit the emergency room, mostly for IV fluids until the virus runs its course. The vaccine information sheet for rotavirus mentions twenty to sixty deaths a year from the disease in the United States, so a death from rotavirus dehydration is an incredibly rare event.

Worldwide, however, where medical care is not adequate, hundreds of thousands of children die from dehydration from rotavirus each year. If IV fluids are not available, a child becomes severely dehydrated and dies before the body can recover.

How is rotavirus transmitted and how likely is my child to get rotavirus?

Rotavirus is transmitted orally, meaning that some-one touches something that has the virus on it and then touches their mouth or eats some food. This is very common in day cares where the staff has to change many diapers a day. Unfortunately, rotavirus is very hardy and is not usually killed by normal hand-washing routines. This makes it very easily spread, and almost all children will have at least one infection before the age of five. The virus is most common in the winter and early spring, between November and May.

What kind of vaccine for rotavirus exists and when is it usually given?

There are two oral rotavirus vaccines available in 2008. RotaTeq is given at two, four, and six months of age and is not approved for children over thirty-two weeks old. RotaRix is given at two and four months of age and is not approved for children over twenty-four weeks old. Even though rotavirus afflicts older children, the most severe cases of dehydration occur in young infants, which is why the vaccine is focused on that age group.

How effective is the rotavirus vaccine?

While not perfect, both vaccines protect against severe rotavirus disease. That means that children who are vaccinated are less likely to require emergency room visits or hospitalizations for treatment of diarrhea. The range of protection is from 75 to 95 percent depending on the study, and it seems the protection lasts for more than just one rotavirus season.

How serious and how common are the side effects of the rotavirus vaccine?

The most common mild side effect is diarrhea. Children who receive the vaccine have a very slight increase (less than 5 percent) in risk of developing diarrhea. There have been no moderate or serious side effects from the vaccine.

A previous rotavirus vaccine named RotaShield was withdrawn from the market in the late 1990s, when it was found that it was associated with a very slight increase in the incidence of intussusception. Intussusception is a rare large-bowel complication in which loops of bowel collapse into each other like a telescope. This problem can occur naturally, but it occurred slightly more frequently after the RotaShield vaccine. The current vaccines are being carefully monitored for an increased rate of intussusception, and none has been found to date.

What are the medical reasons to not give the rotavirus vaccine?

The rotavirus vaccine should not be given to anyone who has had a severe allergic reaction to a previous dose of the vaccine or to any component in the vaccine. In addition, children who are moderately or severely ill should be cautioned against receiving this vaccine until they recover from their illness.

Because the vaccine contains a live, attenuated virus, it is not recommended for any person with a deficiency of the immune system. This would include anyone who has HIV or certain kinds of cancer, is receiving chemotherapy or radiation therapy, or has been on medications that suppress the immune system, such as steroids, for more than two weeks.

Although the current rotavirus vaccines have not been associated with an increased risk of intussusception, any child who has had an intussusception is at higher risk of having a repeat episode in the future. Thus, any child who has had an intussusception in the past should not receive a rotavirus vaccine.

The rotavirus vaccine is only approved for children from six weeks of age to either twenty-four or thirty-two weeks of age (depending on the brand).

What is Dr. Jamie's overall recommendation for the rotavirus vaccine?

The rotavirus vaccine is more important than it may seem. At first glance, diarrhea seems like a rather minor problem. Although every child will likely get rotavirus in the first two years of life, most are able to weather it easily at home. However, over fifty thousand children a year are hospitalized because of the disease. In addition, the vaccine is simple, is orally administered so it doesn't hurt, and has minimal side effects. Given this combination, I put the rotavirus vaccine on my second tier of recommendations. It is not as important as HiB, pneumococcus, or pertussis, which can have permanent effects, but it is important.

Chapter 10 THE INFLUENZA VACCINE

- What is influenza and what kind of problems does it cause?
- How serious and how treatable is the influenza infection?
- How is influenza transmitted and how likely is my child to get influenza?
- What kind of vaccine for influenza exists and when is it usually given?
- How effective is the influenza vaccine?
- How serious and how common are the side effects of the influenza vaccine?
- What are the medical reasons to not give the influenza vaccine?
- What is Dr. Jamie's overall recommendation for the influenza vaccine?

What is influenza and what kind of problems does it cause?

Influenza is a virus that usually leads to respiratory symptoms, such as a cough and a runny nose. However, it is also associated with other symptoms, such as a high fever, chills, muscle aches, and general fatigue.

How serious and how treatable is the influenza infection?

For healthy people, influenza can be severe but not life threatening. However, even healthy young adults can be sick enough to be in bed for a week with a high fever and muscle aches. When we get a cold or feverish illness in the winter, we generally talk about being sick with "the flu." For those who have had an actual bout of influenza, the comparison between "the flu" and the real influenza virus is like the difference between falling off your bike and being hit by a truck. I have had people with the influenza virus tell me that it hurts to open their eyes!

The major risk of influenza is that it can make an underlying disease worse. So if you have diabetes or asthma or a heart condition, being sick with influenza can exacerbate those illnesses. In addition, influenza can predispose you to other infections, such as bacterial pneumonia. So while the influenza virus might not kill you, the resulting complications might. The current estimates are that over thirty-six thousand people die each year from complications of influenza. Of that number, less than a hundred are children, so the vast majority of deaths are in adults.

There are antiviral medicines available that shorten the course and decrease the severity of the illness. In addition, they also reduce the spread of the virus to uninfected people. Unfortunately, they need to be started within forty-eight hours of the start of symptoms to be effective. In addition, they are expensive and only shorten the course of the illness by one to two days. Furthermore, some strains of the virus have become resistant to certain medicines, limiting your doctor's choices. In general, these medicines are recommended more for people who are at high risk of complications from influenza than for otherwise healthy individuals.

How is influenza transmitted and how likely is my child to get influenza?

Influenza is a respiratory infection and is transmitted by droplets or by direct contact with objects that have been touched by droplets. Common sense precautions, such as hand washing and avoiding others who are coughing, are an excellent way to avoid getting sick with this illness. Outbreaks of influenza occur during the winter, and the flu season is thought to be active starting in October or November and lasting until March or April in the Northern Hemisphere. The flu season is reversed below the equator, which might be relevant for those traveling below the equator between May and October.

The most critical fact to understand about influenza is that there will be millions of cases each winter. Millions of cases. This is the most common infection for which there is a vaccine, and it is very likely your child will be exposed. Statistically, children are more likely than adults to catch influenza in any given season. This is probably related to their close contact with sick classmates at school. However, children under age five and adults are more likely to be hospitalized than school-aged children.

What kind of vaccine for influenza exists and when is it usually given?

There are two kinds of influenza vaccine: a killed virus vaccine that is given by injection and a live virus vaccine that is given using a spray in the nose. The vaccine is recommended during flu season, which starts every fall in October in the United

States. However, you can still receive the vaccination as late as early spring if the flu season lasts longer than usual.

The flu vaccine is recommended annually for all children ages six months to eighteen years, for all adults over age fifty, and for all other individuals at higher risk of developing complications from influenza. That includes people who have chronic heart, lung, or kidney disease, people with diabetes or immune deficiencies, and women who are pregnant. Note that the previous recommendation for healthy children was only for children ages six months to five years, but in 2008, the recommendation was changed to include all children. Children under nine years of age should receive two doses of the flu vaccine, one month apart, during the first flu season in which they receive the vaccine.

The live-virus nasal-spray vaccine is the more limited of the two types of influenza vaccines. It is only approved for people ages two to forty-nine and should not be given to people who are allergic to eggs, who are on aspirin therapy, or who have asthma. In addition, it should be given cautiously, if at all, to someone who has had Guillain-Barré syndrome (GBS) or to children who have recurrent wheezing. It is also not recommended for people with diseases such as diabetes or chronic illnesses of the heart, lung, or kidneys, or anyone with a weak immune system.

The killed-virus version of the flu vaccine comes in many different forms from many different manufacturers. Some are only for children over four years old; some are approved for children as young as six months old. Some versions contain thimerosal, a mercury derivative (see page 256 for more details on this ingredient), and some are thimerosal-free. In the end, however, there is an injectable version of the influenza vaccine for everyone over six months of age.

How effective is the influenza vaccine?

The effectiveness of the influenza vaccine varies from year to year. Each year the vaccine contains only the three strains of influenza that researchers feel are mostly likely to be circulating in the upcoming flu season. The decision on which strains to include has to be made months in advance in order to produce the millions of doses required. Sometimes the experts make a wrong choice, and the viral strains in the vaccine do not exactly match the strains in the community. Thus, the effectiveness of the vaccine can vary from 50 percent to over 95 percent depending on the match.

How serious and how common are the side effects of the influenza vaccine?

The majority of side effects from the vaccines are mild. The live-virus nasal flu vaccine has a risk of giving you a runny nose and congestion as well as a fever and muscle aches. This makes sense because you are getting a weakened form of the virus and you might get a mild influenza infection. The injectable version of the vaccine can occasionally cause a sore arm or swelling and redness at the injection site.

A different version of the flu vaccine was linked to Guillain-Barré syndrome (GBS) during the 1970s. The current version is not linked to GBS. However, as a precaution, people who have had GBS should discuss the risks and benefits of the vaccine with their doctor.

What are the medical reasons to not give the influenza vaccine?

The flu vaccine should not be given to anyone who has had a severe allergic reaction to a previous dose of the vaccine or to any component in the vaccine, including egg protein. In addition, people who are moderately or severely ill should be cautioned against receiving this vaccine until they recover from their illness. If you have ever had Guillain-Barré syndrome, you should discuss the pros and cons of receiving the flu vaccine with your physician.

Because the nasal-spray vaccine contains a live, attenuated virus, it is not recommended for any person with a deficiency of the immune system. This would include anyone who has HIV or certain kinds of cancer, is receiving chemotherapy or radiation therapy, or has been on medications that suppress the immune system, such as steroids, for more than two weeks. It is also not recommended for anyone who is pregnant or might be getting pregnant.

In addition to these recommendations, anyone who has certain chronic medical conditions, such as asthma or other lung disease, heart or kidney disease, diabetes, or sickle cell disease, should not receive the live-flu-virus nasal-spray vaccine. Finally, children on long-term aspirin therapy should also not receive the nasal-spray vaccine.

The inactivated, injectable vaccine is approved for anyone over six months old. The live-flu-virus nasal-spray vaccine is approved for anyone between the ages of two and fifty years.

What is Dr. Jamie's overall recommendation for the influenza vaccine?

The flu is a very common illness, and it is likely that your child will be exposed to it several times in his or her life, if not every year. Fortunately, this illness is rarely life-threatening in children, but it can lead to hospitalization in certain circumstances. The side effects are usually mild. I recommend this vaccine mainly because influenza is so common. Not only will it help your child when he or she is exposed, but it will also help prevent the spread of the illness to others who are at higher risk of complications.

Chapter 11

THE HEPATITIS B VACCINE

- What is hepatitis B and what kind of problems does it cause?
- How serious and how treatable is the hepatitis B infection?
- How is hepatitis B transmitted and how likely is my child to get hepatitis B?
- What kind of vaccine for hepatitis B exists and when is it usually given?
- How effective is the hepatitis B vaccine?
- How serious and how common are the side effects of the hepatitis B vaccine?
- What are the medical reasons to not give the hepatitis B vaccine?
- What is Dr. Jamie's overall recommendation for the hepatitis B vaccine?

What is hepatitis B and what kind of problems does it cause?

Hepatitis B is a virus that infects and attacks the liver. Many people are exposed to the virus at some time in their lives and are able to fight the acute infection off completely with no complications or only mild, temporary symptoms. However, some people are unable to eradicate the virus and become chronically infected. They have the hepatitis B virus in the body for the rest of their lives. This latter group of people is called chronic hepatitis B carriers and can spread the virus to other people. In addition, over many years, the chronic infection may damage the liver and lead to liver failure. In certain circumstances, the virus can also lead to liver cancer.

How serious and how treatable is the hepatitis B infection?

There are only a few antiviral treatments for hepatitis B and the success rate for treatment is not good. The side effects of the treatments are common and debilitating and, for some of the treatments, there is a risk that the symptoms will become worse after the antiviral medicine is stopped. This is clearly a disease that is better to prevent than to get.

As for the seriousness of the infection, that depends on the age at which your child catches the disease. Children who are exposed at birth have a 90 percent chance of becoming chronic carriers. These are the children who have the highest risk of developing liver cancer or liver failure when they become young adults. In comparison, adults only have a 10 percent chance of becoming a chronic carrier. Older children have a lower risk of becoming a chronic carrier than newborns but a higher risk than adults.

How is hepatitis B transmitted and how likely is my child to get hepatitis B?

Hepatitis B is a blood-borne virus, and thus, the only way to get the disease is to be exposed to the blood of someone who is a carrier. The most common way that children become infected is during childbirth. If the mother is a hepatitis B carrier, she can transfer the virus to the baby at birth. Fortunately, in most countries, pregnant women are routinely tested for this virus during their pregnancy. If a woman is found to be a carrier, the baby receives both a vaccine and a special immune globulin that contains antibodies against hepatitis B. This decreases the baby's risk of acquiring the infection.

Other methods of spreading this disease include sexual intercourse and IV drug use. A blood transfusion is another method of transmission, but because the blood supply is screened, the risk there is very low. Finally, direct exposure to the blood of a carrier can transmit this infection. Thus, if your child is exposed to a bleeding cut of another child who is a carrier and that blood touches your child's blood (through an open wound or via mucus membranes like the mouth), then your child could become infected.

Overall, your baby's risk of being exposed to this virus is low. Almost all mothers are screened during pregnancy, and most infants do not have as many risk factors as adults.

What kind of vaccine for hepatitis B exists and when is it usually given?

The hepatitis B vaccine is a recombinant vaccine. This means that yeast cells are used to duplicate a protein on the outer wall of the hepatitis B virus. This protein is filtered out of the solution and used in the vaccine. There is no way that someone can become infected with the virus because only the capsule protein is used as the immune-system stimulant. However, this process does make it more likely that someone with an allergy to yeast might have a reaction to the vaccine.

There are many different schedules for the hepatitis B vaccine. One common schedule is to give the first dose at birth, the second one month later, and the third dose six months after the first dose. This is also an acceptable schedule for adults. Another common schedule is to give the three doses at birth, two, and six months of age.

One important detail is that children who are born to mothers who are hepatitis B carriers need to get the vaccine within twelve hours of birth. At the same time, they will receive a dose of hepatitis B immune globulin (HBIG), which contains antibodies against the virus. This combination of vaccine and HBIG dramatically decreases the risk that the baby will contract hepatitis B from its mother.

How effective is the hepatitis B vaccine?

The hepatitis B vaccine is very effective, with over 99 percent of children protected after three doses. There do appear to be some people who do not respond to the vaccine, even after multiple series of vaccines. Some research suggests a genetic basis for this inability to produce hepatitis B antibodies.

The duration of protection from the vaccination is still being studied. In some studies, the protection lasts for over ten years. However, other studies suggest that a significant minority of children, maybe up to 40 percent, have waning immunity as they reach adolescence. Even with the waning immunity, though, it is uncommon to find vaccinated individuals becoming infected with hepatitis B. For that reason, no booster doses have been recommended. The expert thinking is that our measure of immunity is not sensitive enough to evaluate the true protective effect of the vaccine.

How serious and how common are the side effects of the hepatitis B vaccine?

The hepatitis B vaccine is a very benign vaccine. The common side effects, such as soreness and fever, are mild and transient. The severe side effects, such as allergic reaction, are rare at less than one in a million cases.

There has been a great deal of research on the possible link between the hepatitis B vaccine and autoimmune diseases. The hepatitis B package insert mentions possible side effects, such as Guillain-Barré syndrome and multiple sclerosis, but then goes on to say that it is unclear if these side effects are vaccine related or just coincidental. Large research studies have also failed to find a link.

What are the medical reasons to not give the hepatitis B vaccine?

The hepatitis B vaccine should not be given to anyone who has had a severe allergic reaction to a previous dose of the vaccine or to any component in the vaccine, including yeast. In addition, people who are moderately or severely ill should be cautioned against receiving this vaccine until they recover from their illness. There are also different rules for administering the hepatitis B vaccine to premature infants, which you should discuss with your baby's doctor. Otherwise, there are no medical reasons to not give this vaccine.

What is Dr. Jamie's overall recommendation for the hepatitis B vaccine?

I strongly recommend the hepatitis B vaccine for teenagers. Even though we hope our children will not become sexually active or use IV drugs, the fact is that some teenagers and young adults do experiment with risky behaviors. And even if your child doesn't, his or her first sexual partner might have experimented in the past. Thus, they will be at risk. If we are able to vaccinate all teenagers over a twenty-year period, we will greatly decrease the transmission of this disease because the teens and twenties are the era of highest risk.

However, the public health argument is to vaccinate all infants. This is based on several lines of thought. First, it is difficult to get teenagers in the doctor's office for vaccines. Infants are clearly a captive population, and the general idea is to give the vaccines when you have someone in your office.

Second, even though all women are tested during pregnancy to see if they are a hepatitis B carrier, sometimes mistakes happen. The wrong test might be ordered, or the wrong result might be written down. Or possibly one of the parents has an affair and contracts hepatitis B during the mother's pregnancy, after the carrier test was done. Thus, it is possible for a mother to be a hepatitis B carrier without knowing it. Public health officials believe it is better to immunize all children at birth in order to avoid missing the one child who particularly needs the vaccine.

Finally, some children do contract hepatitis B from accidental contact with an infected person's blood. These instances are rare but have occurred. The vaccine would protect against these accidents.

My attitude is that the vaccine is a good idea for both the public health and the individual protection of your child. However, it is not a critical vaccine for infants, as they are unlikely to be exposed in the first several years of life. So if I have parents who are hesitant about vaccines, it is not at the top of my list, and I am comfortable putting it off until age eleven.

Having said that, the hepatitis B vaccine is now required for admission to many schools and day cares. Thus, you might need to give it earlier than you were hoping. In addition, hepatitis B is now part of many common combination vaccines, which means fewer injections for your child if you follow the recommended vaccine schedule. For these reasons, many parents just go with the path of least resistance and give the vaccine to their infants.

Chapter 12 THE POLIO VACCINE

- What is polio and what kind of problems does it cause?
- How serious and how treatable is the polio infection?
- How is polio transmitted and how likely is my child to get polio?
- What kind of vaccine for polio exists and when is it usually given?
- How effective is the polio vaccine?
- How serious and how common are the side effects of the polio vaccine?
- What are the medical reasons to not give the polio vaccine?
- What is Dr. Jamie's overall recommendation for the polio vaccine?

What is polio and what kind of problems does it cause?

When we think of polio, we usually think of children in braces or requiring a iron lung to breathe. However, the vast majority of poliovirus infections have no symptoms at all. Less than 10 percent have a minor illness with a fever or sore throat. Less than 5 percent have a mild case of meningitis, and around 1 percent have the full-fledged paralysis of certain muscles (poliomyelitis). Only about a third of those with paralysis recover completely.

How serious and how treatable is the polio infection?

If you happen to develop paralysis from polio, it is a very serious infection. If the muscles affected are involved with respiration, you could die without breathing assistance. In the past, that involved an iron lung, but now you would require a ventilator. If other muscles, such as an arm or leg, are involved, you might require a brace or a walker for the rest of your life. Unfortunately, there is no treatment for paralytic polio once it has occurred.

How is polio transmitted and how likely is my child to get polio?

Polio is interesting in that it is transmitted both via coughs and oral secretions as well as through stools. Luckily, it is almost impossible for your child to be exposed to polio in the United States. The last wild case of poliomyelitis in the United States was in 1979, and the last vaccine-associated case was in 2000. On a global basis, there are still around two thousand wild-virus cases of paralytic polio annually. There are rare reports of the wild virus arriving in the United States, imported by an unimmunized child, but fortunately, none of those episodes has turned into a full-blown case of paralytic poliomyelitis.

What kind of vaccine for polio exists and when is it usually given?

The only approved polio vaccine in the United States is an injectable vaccine. An oral polio vaccine was discontinued in 2000. The oral vaccine contained a weakened virus, which rarely led to the full-blown paralytic poliomyelitis. The injectable vaccine contains a killed virus, and it is impossible to get polio from that vaccine. The polio vaccine can be given separately or in a combination vaccine with other vaccines.

The recommended dosing schedule for the polio vaccine is two and four months, with another dose at six to eighteen months and a booster dose at four to six years. In addition, adult travelers to areas of the world where polio is still common are recommended to get a booster dose. The two countries with the most cases in recent years have been India and Nigeria, but many countries in Asia and Africa have had some cases.

How effective is the polio vaccine?

The polio vaccine is very effective, with over 99 percent of recipients developing protective antibodies. The protection lasts for years and possibly for life.

How serious and how common are the side effects of the polio vaccine?

The only listed side effect of the polio vaccine on the Vaccine Information Sheet is a sore arm. No severe side effects are noted.

What are the medical reasons to not give the polio vaccine?

The polio vaccine should not be given to anyone who has had a severe allergic reaction to a previous dose of the vaccine or to any component in the vaccine, including the following three antibiotics: neomycin, streptomycin, and polymyxin B. In addition, people who are moderately or severely ill are cautioned against receiving this vaccine until they recover from their illness. Otherwise there is no medical reason to not give the polio vaccine.

What is Dr. Jamie's overall recommendation for the polio vaccine?

Polio is a classic public health vaccine. The chance that your child will be exposed to polio while living in the United States is almost zero, and for that reason, the vaccine is not critical in my opinion. For parents who are generally hesitant about vaccines, polio is the least important vaccine on the list. However, part of the reason the risk is so low is that the vaccine is so effective and so many people are protected that our country has excellent herd immunity. To help preserve that herd immunity until the virus has been eradicated from earth, I do recommend the vaccine. I look forward to the day when polio, like smallpox, will be a disease of the past.

Part III
Other Childhood Vaccines

The following chapters focus on vaccines that are recommended for children over the age of one year and for adults in certain circumstances. Remember, if you don't have any concerns about vaccines, I recommend all the vaccines listed. I feel that the benefits outweigh the risks, both for the individual and for society as a whole. However, if you have some specific concerns, you can use the following questions to help you evaluate the risks and benefits of a given vaccine.

- What is disease X and what kind of problems does it cause?
- How serious and how treatable is the disease X infection?
- How is disease X transmitted and how likely is my child to get disease X?
- What kind of vaccine for disease X exists and when is it usually given?
- How effective is the disease X vaccine?

- How serious and how common are the side effects of the disease X vaccine?
- What are the medical reasons to not give the disease X vaccine?
- What is Dr. Jamie's overall recommendation for the disease X vaccine?

Chapter 13 THE MEASLES, MUMPS, AND RUBELLA (MMR) VACCINE

- What are measles, mumps, and rubella and what kind of problems do they cause?
- How serious and how treatable are measles, mumps, and rubella infections?
- How are measles, mumps, and rubella transmitted and how likely is my child to get one of these illnesses?
- What kind of vaccines for measles, mumps, and rubella exist and when are they usually given?
- How effective is the MMR vaccine?
- How serious and how common are the side effects of the MMR vaccine?
- What are the medical reasons to not give the MMR vaccine?
- What is Dr. Jamie's overall recommendation for the MMR vaccine?

What are measles, mumps, and rubella and what kind of problems do they cause?

Measles, mumps, and rubella are illnesses caused by viruses. The most severe of the three is measles. It is characterized by a high fever (often up to 104°F) and a rash. Complications of measles include ear infections, pneumonias, and encephalitis (inflammation of the brain).

Mumps is a milder illness that usually causes swelling of the salivary glands, especially the parotid glands in the mouth that produce saliva. The swelling of the parotid glands gives a person with mumps the classic "chipmunk" face. In men, swelling of the testicles (orchitis) may also occur, which rarely leads to sterility.

Rubella, or German measles, is the mildest illness of the three. It usually causes a low-grade fever, a generalized rash, and some swelling of lymph nodes. Occasionally, adults will have temporary arthritis associated with their infection. The major issue with this illness is that if a pregnant woman develops rubella during pregnancy, she may suffer from a miscarriage or stillbirth, or the baby may suffer from significant birth defects.

How serious and how treatable are measles, mumps, and rubella infections?

Measles can be very serious. It has the highest fever of the three illnesses and makes children the sickest. Even if they don't end up in the hospital from the illness, infected children spend the week in bed, laid low by the virus. Severe complications include encephalitis and pneumonia. The risk of severe brain damage from encephalitis is one in a thousand cases. Death from measles occurs in one to three in a thousand cases, with the patient dying either from encephalitis or pneumonia.

There is no specific treatment for measles, and thus, the medical community must provide supportive care until the body recovers on its own. This might include IV fluids and nutrition, oxygen, and even breathing tubes for severe lung infections. There is a recommendation for vitamin A supplementation in certain circumstances, based on limited data that suggest that the supplement decreases the severity of illness and risk of death.

Mumps is a less severe illness and is less severe in children than in adults. Most of the severe complications, such as swelling of the testicles (orchitis) and sterility, occur in adults. The death rate is lower than measles, about two in ten thousand cases, with the majority of deaths occurring in adults. If a pregnant mother develops a mumps infection during the first three months of pregnancy, she has a slightly increased risk of a miscarriage, but there is no increased risk of birth defects. Like measles, there is no specific treatment for the illness, and the care is merely supportive.

Rubella is a very mild illness for the recipient, with only a mild rash, fever, and swollen lymph nodes for most patients. There are no reports of death from the virus. The major concern with rubella is that a pregnant mother who develops rubella can suffer a miscarriage, stillbirth, or fetal birth defects. Once again, there is no treatment for rubella, merely supportive care.

How are measles, mumps, and rubella transmitted and how likely is my child to get one of these illnesses?

All three illnesses are spread via direct contact with infected secretions or droplets spread by a cough or sneeze. Interestingly, humans are the only known hosts for all three viruses. This means that with enough effort to vaccinate or quarantine the illnesses, theoretically they can be wiped off the face of the earth just like smallpox.

Thanks to the vaccines and herd immunity, all three illnesses are rarely seen in the United States. Annually, there are usually less than five hundred reported cases and sometimes less than a hundred reported cases of all three illnesses combined. Almost all of these illnesses can be traced back to an unimmunized international traveler who brought the virus back to the United States from a foreign country. The virus then spread to either unimmunized individuals or people for whom the immunity from the vaccination had worn off.

The largest recent epidemic for one of these diseases occurred in 2005 and 2006 among college-age students. There were over five thousand cases of mumps in several states, centered mostly on college campuses in the Midwestern United States. That epidemic has receded, and the rate of mumps in the United States has returned to its normal low rate.

However, in countries where public health is not well funded and vaccines are not commonly available to the population, all three illnesses are very common. For example, millions of cases of measles occur yearly, with hundreds of thousands of deaths. If you are considering traveling to a country with a high incidence of any one of these three illnesses, speak to your healthcare provider about ways to decrease your risk of infection.

What kind of vaccines for measles, mumps, and rubella exist and when are they usually given?

The measles, mumps, and rubella vaccines are all attenuated, live-virus vaccines. This means that the virus in the vaccine is weakened but alive and theoretically can give the actual disease to the recipient. This happens very rarely, and when it occurs, the illness is usually milder than when the person is exposed to the wild virus.

While there are three separate vaccines for measles, mumps, and rubella, the most common form of the vaccine given is known as the MMR vaccine, which combines all three vaccines into one dose. The primary benefit of the combination vaccine is receiving one shot instead of three separate shots. As of January 2009, the manufacturer of these vaccines has stopped production and sales of the single component measles, mumps, and rubella vaccines and will only be producing the combined MMR vaccine. Thus, after the current stocks of the single component vaccines have been used up, it will no longer be possible to divide the MMR vaccine into three separate injections.

The MMR vaccine is recommended for all children at age one year, and a booster dose is recommended at age four to six years, usually just before entering kindergarten. If children between six and twelve months of age are traveling to an area of the world with an increased rate of measles, they should receive either the measles vaccine alone, or the MMR combination vaccine, in order to give them some protection while traveling. However, this dose will not count as one of the two doses of measles that is required for school or college; only doses after twelve months of age count for those requirements.

How effective is the MMR vaccine?

The measles vaccine is over 95 percent effective after the first dose and over 99 percent effective after the second dose. This means that over 99 percent of recipients of both doses develop antibodies that prevent infection when exposed to the virus in the community.

The mumps vaccine is less effective, with over 80 percent of recipients protected after one dose and over 90 percent protected after a second dose. The rubella vaccine effectiveness is in the middle, with 95 percent of recipients protected after a single dose.

How serious and how common are the side effects of the MMR vaccine?

Most of the side effects are mild and transient. About 10 to 15 percent of recipients develop a fever, and fewer recipients develop a rash, swollen glands, or joint pains. A scarier side effect is the one in three thousand risk of a seizure. Fortunately, the seizure is also transient and not likely to lead to long-term consequences like epilepsy.

Another rare complication of the vaccine is a temporary low platelet count. Platelets are cells that help prevent bleeding, so it is possible to have problems stopping bleeding when the platelets are low. This complication occurs in about one out of thirty thousand doses.

There have been some cases of encephalitis after the MMR vaccine, but it is unclear if they were due to the vaccine or not. There is a natural background rate of encephalitis in the general population, even when no vaccines are given and it is not clear that the vaccine added to the background rate. In other words, the cases of encephalitis may have been coincidental and not caused by the vaccine. However, the MMR product insert says that the "data suggest the possibility that some of these cases may have been caused by measles vaccines." Even if this is true, though, the estimated risk of one in a million is much less than the risk of encephalitis from the disease (one in a thousand).

There has been much fanfare about the MMR vaccine increasing the risk of autism. I cover this topic more thoroughly in chapter 23, but in brief, many well-respected studies find no link between the MMR vaccine and autism when looked at on a population basis. Whether certain individuals are particularly susceptible is another question, but on a statistical basis, I am comfortable that there is no increased risk.

What are the medical reasons to not give the MMR vaccine?

The MMR vaccine should not be given to anyone who has had a severe allergic reaction to a previous dose of the vaccine or to any component in the vaccine, including gelatin or the antibiotic neomycin. In addition, people who are moderately or severely ill should be cautioned against receiving this vaccine until they recover from their illness.

Pregnant women should wait until after their pregnancy to receive the vaccine to avoid the theoretical risk of infecting the fetus with the live virus. Women who are not pregnant should wait until at least four weeks after receiving the MMR vaccine before becoming pregnant.

Because the vaccine contains a live, attenuated virus, it is not recommended for any person with a deficiency of the immune system. This would include anyone who has HIV or certain kinds of cancer, is receiving chemotherapy or radiation therapy, or has been on medications that suppress the immune system, such as steroids, for more than two weeks.

People who have a history of a low platelet count should discuss with their doctors the risks and benefits of receiving the MMR vaccine because one of the rare side effects of the vaccine is to lower a recipient's platelet count.

People who have received a blood transfusion or other blood products, such as immune globulin, should usually wait before receiving the MMR vaccine. The waiting period ranges from three to eleven months, depending on the type and volume of blood products received.

What is Dr. Jamie's overall recommendation for the MMR vaccine?

I recommend this vaccine, but I can also understand when parents are hesitant to administer this vaccine to their children. Measles, mumps, and rubella are not common in the United States, and if you believe in the potential side effect of autism (which I don't), that is a scary threat. In my office I provide the opportunity to receive the measles, mumps, and rubella vaccines separately if parents feel strongly about the issue. However, as previously mentioned, the manufacturer has stopped producing the single component vaccines as of January 2009, so that option will no longer be available.

I strongly recommend the vaccine for any travelers to countries with an increased incidence of measles, mumps, or rubella. I also strongly recommend that women receive the rubella vaccine before becoming sexually active. Finally, I recommend the mumps vaccine before adolescence because the disease is worse as a teenager or adult than as a child.

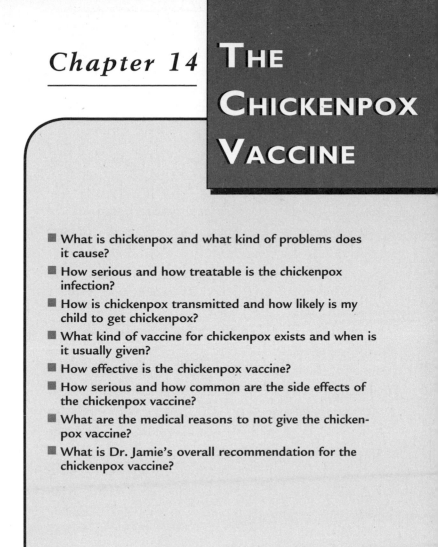

Chapter 14

THE CHICKENPOX VACCINE

- What is chickenpox and what kind of problems does it cause?
- How serious and how treatable is the chickenpox infection?
- How is chickenpox transmitted and how likely is my child to get chickenpox?
- What kind of vaccine for chickenpox exists and when is it usually given?
- How effective is the chickenpox vaccine?
- How serious and how common are the side effects of the chickenpox vaccine?
- What are the medical reasons to not give the chickenpox vaccine?
- What is Dr. Jamie's overall recommendation for the chickenpox vaccine?

What is chickenpox and what kind of problems does it cause?

Chickenpox, also known as varicella, usually causes a mild infection with a fever and a whole-body rash of hundreds of itchy lesions. Before the vaccine, almost every child in the United States contracted the disease. Chickenpox is extremely contagious, with the vast majority of unimmunized household contacts developing the disease after exposure.

How serious and how treatable is the chickenpox infection?

In general, chickenpox is a mild illness. The vast majority of infected individuals stay out of school or work for about seven to ten days with annoying symptoms such as fever and itching. However, chickenpox tends to be worse in adolescents and adults, as well as in individuals with a weakened immune system, who have a higher risk of complications such as encephalitis and pneumonia. Even healthy individuals can develop secondary skin infections from scratching at the chickenpox lesions and allowing bacteria under the skin.

Another group of people who have an increased risk of complications are pregnant women and their newborn babies. There is a slight risk of birth defects for women who develop chickenpox in the first half of pregnancy. Even worse, there is increased risk of neonatal death if the mother develops chickenpox within a week of delivery.

Cases of death related to chickenpox are rare. Before the vaccine was regularly administered, millions of children developed the disease in the United States every year, and around ten thousand people were hospitalized, but only 150 people died of complications. Even though most of the cases of chickenpox occurred in children, most of the deaths were in adults because they had a more severe case of the disease. Since the vaccine, the number of cases of chickenpox and the number of hospitalizations and deaths have declined. This is an example of decreasing the complications and deaths from a disease by making the disease less common in the community.

There are antiviral treatments for chickenpox, but they are usually only recommended for individuals at higher risk of complications, such as pregnant women and people with weakened immune systems. These medicines should be started within seventy-two hours of the first skin lesion. In addition, if a high-risk person has been exposed, he or she can receive the vaccine (if not previously immunized) or varicella-zoster immune globulin (VZIG), a compound that contains antibodies to the virus that might prevent the disease from taking hold.

How is chickenpox transmitted and how likely is my child to get chickenpox?

Chickenpox is transmitted when a person comes in contact with secretions from the mouth or eye of an infected individual. Occasionally there is airborne spread caused by droplets from coughing or sneezing. Rarely, a person can acquire the disease from direct contact with shingles skin lesions. Shingles, also known as herpes zoster, is a reactivation of the chickenpox virus later in life. (See chapter 20 for more information on shingles.)

With the advent of the chickenpox vaccine, it is becoming less likely for a child to develop chickenpox from exposure in the community; there is simply less of it around. Parents and physicians have all noticed a marked decline in the frequency of the disease. Even so, it is still much more prevalent than measles, mumps, or rubella, which are very rare.

What kind of vaccine for chickenpox exists and when is it usually given?

The chickenpox vaccine is another live-virus vaccine. This means that it is possible to get the actual disease from the vaccine, albeit a milder case than that obtained from the community. Because it can possibly lead to an actual infection, the chickenpox vaccine should not be administered to pregnant women or people who have a compromised immune system.

The recommended schedule for the chickenpox vaccine is the first dose at twelve to fifteen months of age and a booster at four to six years, usually before entering kindergarten. There is some evidence that the vaccine is slightly more effective if given at fifteen months instead of at twelve months of age.

It used to be thought that a single dose of the vaccine was sufficient, but recent evidence has shown that about 15 percent of recipients are not fully protected after one dose. Thus, children over age six who only received one dose in the past should receive a booster dose at any time. The second dose has always been recommended for teenagers and adults.

How effective is the chickenpox vaccine?

The two-dose series is extremely effective, with over 99 percent of recipients fully protected against the virus. However, part of the effectiveness of the vaccine in the past was due to regular reexposure to the wild virus in the community. In essence, being exposed to another person in the community with chickenpox was like getting a booster dose of the vaccine.

With the number of cases of community-acquired chickenpox decreasing, there is some concern that additional booster doses will be necessary in the future. This has already occurred with the recommendation changing from one dose at twelve to fifteen months to include a booster dose at kindergarten. Because widespread vaccination did not start until the late 1990s, it is unclear whether the chickenpox will just require two doses, like the MMR vaccine, or whether boosters will be needed every ten years, like the tetanus vaccine. Only time will tell.

Another question about the vaccine is whether or not it will protect against shingles. This question will take decades to answer. In the past, most cases of chickenpox occurred in childhood, and most cases of shingles occurred in adults over age fifty. Thus, it will take years to decide if the vaccine significantly decreases the risk of shingles.

How serious and how common are the side effects of the chickenpox vaccine?

The side effects of the chickenpox vaccine are mild. About 20 to 30 percent of recipients develop a sore arm from the vaccine. About 10 to 15 percent of recipients develop a fever, but interestingly, the same number of recipients who received a saline injection also developed a fever. This suggests that the vaccine is not the cause of this fever. As always, whenever children develop a fever, a few of them might develop a febrile seizure, a seizure caused by the fever.

In addition, it is possible to actually develop a mild case of chickenpox from the vaccine with an associated rash. Remember, this is milder than the wild-virus case of chickenpox. Finally, there is a rare risk of pneumonia and other severe complications, but again, it is not always clear that the vaccine caused the complication.

What are the medical reasons to not give the chickenpox vaccine?

The chickenpox vaccine should not be given to anyone who has had a severe allergic reaction to a previous dose of the vaccine or to any component in the vaccine, including gelatin or the antibiotic neomycin. In addition, people who are moderately or severely ill should be cautioned against receiving this vaccine until they recover from their illness.

Pregnant women should wait until after their pregnancy to receive the vaccine to avoid the theoretical risk of infecting the fetus with the live virus. Women who are not pregnant should wait until at least four weeks after receiving the MMR vaccine before becoming pregnant.

Because the vaccine contains a live, attenuated virus, it is not recommended for any person with a deficiency of the immune system. This would include anyone who has HIV or certain kinds of cancer, is receiving chemotherapy or radiation therapy, or has been on medications that suppress the immune system, such as steroids, for more than two weeks.

People who have received a blood transfusion or other blood products, such as immune globulin, should usually wait before receiving the MMR vaccine. The waiting period ranges from three to eleven months, depending on the type and volume of blood products received.

What is Dr. Jamie's overall recommendation for the chickenpox vaccine?

This is an example where one needs to weigh the public health benefits of the vaccine against the individual benefits of the vaccine. For a given child, chickenpox is a mild disease, more annoying than deadly. Thus, some parents would prefer to get full immunity from the disease rather the vaccine. In addition, there is the worry about the vaccine wearing off, and then we will find populations of adults getting the disease with their increased risk of complications.

However, from a public health point of view, the benefits of preventing thousands of hospitalizations and dozens of deaths each year is significant. If we can make the disease as rare as measles or mumps, we will have only hundreds of cases a year instead of millions. This will protect those people who are at higher risk of complications from an infection, such as those who are on chemotherapy or women who are pregnant.

I strongly recommend this vaccine for anyone who might need to be on steroids for a chronic disease like asthma. It is clear that people on steroids have a much higher risk of having a severe episode of the illness. Otherwise, my recommendation in favor of the chickenpox vaccine is more from a societal perspective, and I can understand why some parents choose to delay this vaccine.

Chapter 15 THE HEPATITIS A VACCINE

- What is hepatitis A and what kind of problems does it cause?
- How serious and how treatable is the hepatitis A infection?
- How is hepatitis A transmitted and how likely is my child to get hepatitis A?
- What kind of vaccine for hepatitis A exists and when is it usually given?
- How effective is the hepatitis A vaccine?
- How serious and how common are the side effects of the hepatitis A vaccine?
- What are the medical reasons to not give the hepatitis A vaccine?
- What is Dr. Jamie's overall recommendation for the hepatitis A vaccine?

What is hepatitis A and what kind of problems does it cause?

Hepatitis A is a virus that attacks the liver. It usually causes a short-lived illness that includes a fever, a decreased appetite, and occasionally some nausea and vomiting. In addition, it can lead to jaundice, a condition in which the skin turns yellow.

How serious and how treatable is the hepatitis A infection?

Hepatitis A is usually a limited disease. Children can have the illness without even noticing any symptoms, although a few will be mildly ill and even fewer will have jaundice. Adults are more likely to notice the nausea and general malaise, and over half of adults will become jaundiced. When symptoms occur, they can last for several weeks, with very rare cases lasting up to six months.

The major risk of hepatitis A is that the virus will attack the liver so severely that the liver will end up failing and shutting down. This is very rare but is more common in people with preexisting liver disease, such as alcoholics or people already infected with hepatitis C.

There is no specific treatment for either the mild or severe hepatitis A infection. In both cases, the medical community provides supportive care, which might range from rest and fluids all the way up to hospitalization and a possible liver transplant. The good news is that, unlike hepatitis B, there is no chronic hepatitis A. Once the illness is over, there will no longer be any virus remaining in your body.

How is hepatitis A transmitted and how likely is my child to get hepatitis A?

Hepatitis A is transmitted orally, most commonly through food. The virus is shed in the stool and if a person does not wash his or her hands well enough after using the bathroom, that person is able to pass the virus on to someone else. Common situations where the virus is easily spread are in restaurants, in day-care centers where workers have to change diapers, and in many developing countries.

Even in the United States, hepatitis A is not rare. Before the vaccine was commonly used, over twenty-five thousand cases a year were reported to the CDC. This just represented the tip of the iceberg, since so many cases are mild and never even diagnosed. More recently, less than six thousand cases a year were reported to the CDC, suggesting that the immunization program is having an effect.

Thus, hepatitis A is not rare in the United States but is not common either. It is much more common overseas in developing countries, which is why doctors recommend that most oversea travelers receive either the vaccine or immune globulin (see the following question and response).

What kind of vaccine for hepatitis A exists and when is it usually given?

There are two inactivated hepatitis A vaccines available in the United States. Both are available for anyone twelve months of age or older, although adults (over age eighteen) receive a higher dose. The vaccines are recommended for children between one and two years of age, with a booster six months later. In addition, the vaccine is recommended for anyone at risk of contracting hepatitis A, such as an international traveler or someone with preexisting liver disease. Again, there is a recommended booster dose six months later.

There is also an immune globulin that protects against hepatitis A. An immune globulin is a mixture of antibodies that protects against certain diseases, in this case hepatitis A. An immune globulin is useful if you have to protect a child less than twelve months old or if you don't have the two or three weeks of time needed to wait for a vaccine to become effective.

An example of the latter situation would be day-care workers who find that one of the children in their class has just been diagnosed with hepatitis A. Because the virus spreads even before the child becomes ill, the workers have probably already been exposed. If they receive the immune globulin immediately, they have an 85 percent chance of being protected from developing the illness from this exposure. The workers should also receive the vaccine because the benefits of the immune globulin wear off after three to six months.

How effective is the hepatitis A vaccine?

The vaccine is very effective, with over 95 percent of recipients developing appropriate antibodies by one month after the initial dose. After the booster dose, 100 percent of recipients develop appropriate antibodies. The protection lasts for at least ten years and appears to be lifelong.

How serious and how common are the side effects of the hepatitis A vaccine?

The side effects of the vaccine are very mild and only last one to two days. These include soreness, headache, fatigue, and a mild loss of appetite. As always, there is the extremely rare risk of a severe allergic reaction, but that is true for any vaccine.

What are the medical reasons to not give the hepatitis A vaccine?

The hepatitis A vaccine should not be given to anyone who has had a severe allergic reaction to a previous dose of the vaccine or to any component in the vaccine, including alum and 2-phenoxyethanol. In addition, people who are moderately or severely ill should be cautioned against receiving this vaccine until they recover from their illness. Otherwise there is no medical reason to not receive the hepatitis A vaccine.

What is Dr. Jamie's overall recommendation for the hepatitis A vaccine?

I recommend this vaccine, mainly because there are so few side effects and because so many people travel to developing countries at some point in their lives. In addition, even though the CDC recommendation to give this vaccine to one-year-olds is relatively new, the vaccine has been around for years and has been well studied. Finally, the vaccine is now covered by insurance when given to children between one and two years of age. However, it is not always covered by insurance when given to older children or adults so there is an advantage to give the vaccine when recommended.

However, I recognize that the disease is usually unrecognized and mild in most children when symptoms do appear. I also understand that unless you are traveling overseas, the illness is not common for most people in the United States. So for these reasons, I do see why some parents would put this vaccine lower on their list of necessary vaccines.

Chapter 16

THE TETANUS, DIPHTHERIA, AND ACELLULAR PERTUSSIS (TDAP AND TD) VACCINES

The Tdap and Td vaccines and their respective illnesses are more thoroughly discussed in chapter 8 on page 119. In brief, the Tdap vaccine is an adolescent and adult variation of the DTaP vaccine, which is recommended only for children under age seven. The Tdap vaccine differs in that it has less diphtheria toxoid and less pertussis antigen than the DTaP vaccine. This is represented by the little "d" and little "p" in Tdap instead of the capital "D" and capital "P" in DTaP. The Td vaccine is the adolescent and adult tetanus and diphtheria booster that is recommended every ten years.

The Tdap vaccine is recommended for all children eleven to twelve years of age. In addition, it is recommended as a single-dose replacement for the regular Td booster that occurs every ten years. This means that if teenagers or adults are scheduled to receive a tetanus booster because it has been ten years since their last dose, they should now receive the Tdap vaccine instead. After receiving Tdap once, they would then continue with the Td boosters every ten years for the rest of their lives.

Finally, the Tdap vaccine is recommended for any regular caregiver or household contact of a young infant. A major drawback of the DTaP vaccine is that the immunity to pertussis wanes over time, meaning that most adults are no longer protected from whooping cough. Fortunately, adults only have mild symptoms, such as a lingering cough. However, they are still able to pass the infection on to young children who have not yet been immunized. By vaccinating close contacts with a booster dose and making sure siblings are up to date on their DTaP vaccines, parents will decrease the risk of their newborn baby being exposed to whooping cough.

I recommend both the Tdap and Td vaccines. The Tdap has a slightly higher risk of side effects compared to the Td vaccine but a much smaller risk of serious side effects compared to the DTaP vaccine. In addition, I regularly see whooping cough in my community. We usually have an outbreak every other year. Given the prominence and potential significance of the illness, I appreciate any opportunity to protect against this disease.

Chapter 17 THE MENINGOCOCCAL VACCINE

- What is meningococcus and what kind of problems does it cause?
- How serious and how treatable is meningococcal disease?
- How is meningococcal disease transmitted and how likely is my child to get this illness?
- What kind of vaccine for meningococcal disease exists and when is it usually given?
- How effective is the meningococcal disease vaccine?
- How serious and how common are the side effects of the meningococcal disease vaccine?
- What are the medical reasons to not give the meningococcal vaccine?
- What is Dr. Jamie's overall recommendation for the meningococcal vaccine?

What is meningococcus and what kind of problems does it cause?

Meningococcus is another name for the *Neisseria meningitides* bacterium. It is a dangerous bacterium that can lead to sepsis (a bloodstream infection) or meningitis (an infection of the fluid surrounding the brain and spinal fluid) or both. Milder infections can lead to pneumonia or a joint infection.

How serious and how treatable is meningococcal disease?

Meningococcal disease is extremely serious. These are the cases that you hear about where a college student is healthy and walking around campus one day and is dead twenty-four hours later. The fatality rate for this disease is 10 percent overall and up to 25 percent in adolescents. Even in milder cases where patients recover, they still might be left deaf or with other disabilities, or they might need to have parts of their body amputated from gangrene.

There are antibiotics that can treat a meningococcal infection. In fact, the majority of time, simple penicillin is sufficient to kill the bacteria. However, the infection often progresses so rapidly and overwhelms so many of the body organs that antibiotics alone are not sufficient. Other treatments, such as intubation and ventilation to support the lungs and fluids and strong cardiac medications to maintain the blood pressure, might be necessary as well. Even in the best circumstances with immediate diagnosis and excellent care, people can still die from this infection.

How is meningococcal disease transmitted and how likely is my child to get this illness?

Meningococcal bacteria are spread via droplets from the upper respiratory tract. The droplets can be spread by coughing, a runny nose, or direct contact with oral secretions, such as by sharing a toothbrush. Interestingly, some people are colonized with these bacteria, which means that they carry the bacteria in their respiratory tracts but do not become ill. Unfortunately, they are still able to spread the disease to others.

Knowing about these methods of transmission is helpful in determining who should receive preventative antibiotics if they are exposed to someone with serious meningococcal disease. The general rule is that the closer you have been to an infected person, the higher your risk of developing the disease and the more likely you should take the antibiotics. Thus, household contacts, plus nursery-school or day-care contacts, should receive the protective antibiotics. In addition, anyone with direct contact with a person's oral secretions, such as someone who kissed or shared a spoon or fork with an infected person, should also receive the antibiotics. If the infection is caused by a subtype that is part of one of the available vaccines (see the following questions), then exposed individuals should consider receiving the vaccine along with the antibiotics.

In general, meningococcal disease is a random, sporadic event. Only two to three thousand cases occur in the United States every year. Thus, unless your child is exposed to someone with a significant illness, it is a relatively rare disease. However, because it is so dramatic and can strike healthy individuals, it is a fearsome infection for many parents.

What kind of vaccine for meningococcal disease exists and when is it usually given?

There are two types of meningococcal vaccines available in the United States. The older vaccine is a polysaccharide vaccine called MPSV4 and goes by the trade name Menomune. It is recommended for high-risk children two years of age and older. High-risk children include those without a functional spleen or with certain immunodeficiencies.

The second vaccine is a newer polysaccharide vaccine. It is known as MCV4 and goes by the trade name of Menactra. Menactra is at least as effective in preventing meningitis infections as Menomune and possibly lasts longer. The recommendation is to give this vaccine to all children at their eleven- or twelve-year-old well-child checkup, with catch-up doses recommended for older teenagers. In addition, high-risk children from ages two to ten years can also receive Menactra instead of Menomune.

How effective is the meningococcal disease vaccine?

There are at least thirteen subtypes of the meningococcal virus, but only five of them cause the vast majority of serious disease. Both vaccines protect against the same four of the five subtypes. Fortunately, the four subtypes account for the majority of disease in adults and adolescents, while the fifth subtype, serogroup B, accounts for half of the infections in infants.

Thus, the effectiveness of the vaccine depends on which serogroup the patient is exposed to. If the serogroup is in one of the vaccines, then the vaccines will be tremendously helpful, protecting 90 percent of recipients. If it is a different serogroup, the vaccine will not help at all.

The protection from the older Menomune vaccine wanes more quickly than other similar vaccines, often fading after three to five years. The hope is that the newer vaccine, Menactra, will provide more long-lasting protection. However, as it only was approved in 2005, the long-term protection is still unknown.

How serious and how common are the side effects of the meningococcal disease vaccine?

The side effects of the vaccine are common but mild. About 50 percent of recipients will report some sort of problem such as redness, pain, swelling, or fever.

There were several cases of Guillain-Barré syndrome (GBS) in the weeks following the administration of Menactra in 2005. However, there is a low background rate of GBS in the general population. It is not clear if those cases were part of the known background rate or due to the Menactra. Based on that information, the CDC is continuing to monitor for any increased risk of GBS after the administration of Menactra.

What are the medical reasons to not give the meningococcal vaccine?

The meningococcal vaccine should not be given to anyone who has had a severe allergic reaction to a previous dose of the vaccine or to any component in the vaccine, including egg protein. In addition, people who are moderately or severely ill should be cautioned against receiving this vaccine until they recover from their illness. Otherwise there is no medical reason to not receive the hepatitis A vaccine.

What is Dr. Jamie's overall recommendation for the meningococcal vaccine?

I strongly recommend this vaccine. Meningococcal disease is relatively rare, but it is devastating when it occurs. The vaccine side effects are minimal, and the vaccine is covered by insurance for children ages eleven to seventeen.

Chapter 18 THE HUMAN PAPILLOMAVIRUS (HPV) VACCINE

- What is HPV and what kind of problems does it cause?
- How serious and how treatable is the HPV infection?
- How is HPV transmitted and how likely is my child to get HPV?
- What kind of HPV vaccines exist and when are they usually given?
- How effective is the HPV vaccine?
- How serious and how common are the side effects of the HPV vaccine?
- What are the medical reasons to not give the HPV vaccine?
- What is Dr. Jamie's overall recommendation for the HPV vaccine?

What is HPV and what kind of problems does it cause?

HPV is a virus that can cause warts as well as certain kinds of dysplasia (precancerous conditions) and cancers. The warts include the common warts seen on hands and feet as well as rectal or genital warts. HPV is also associated with a number of genital-area lesions, including anal, penile, and vulvar dysplasias and cancers. However, the most common association is the link between HPV and cervical dysplasia and cervical cancer.

How serious and how treatable is the HPV infection?

There are over one hundred types of human papillomaviruses. The majority of them are unimportant because they produce no skin lesions and you never even know that you had an infection. A minority of the various types of HPV cause warts. While warts are contagious and cosmetically unappealing, they are not medically significant. There is no perfect cure for warts, and a large number of treatments have evolved to remove them. The most common treatments each work about 70 percent of the time and include freezing, burning, or cutting the warts off, or using an acid solution to remove the wart. Unfortunately, removing the wart does not necessarily remove the virus hidden in the surrounding skin, so recurrences are common. The good news is that many warts will disappear on their own, even without treatment.

A very few types of HPV are associated with dysplasia and cancer. In the case of anal, vulvar, or penile lesions, there are usually obvious skin changes that are signs of the dysplasia or cancer, and the treatment is either freezing the lesion (cryotherapy) or surgically removing the abnormal skin. While it is never fun to have a precancerous or cancerous lesion, these are relatively mild cancers with a very low chance of spreading elsewhere in the body. Recurrences are common because the virus remains in the surrounding area, so regular monitoring for future lesions is important.

There are four types of HPV that are associated with over 90 percent of cervical cancers: types 16, 18, 31, and 45. Because the cervix is hidden inside the vagina, there is no obvious lesion to warn someone about potential problems. However, regular pap smears, which use a brush to collect cells from the surface of the cervix, provide an opportunity to look for dysplasia or cancer. The current recommendation is that women receive a pap smear every year until they have three normal pap smears in a row and then every two to three years thereafter.

If a pap smear demonstrates dysplasia, there are many treatments available. One is simply to closely follow the lesion. A large number of the mild dysplasias and even some of the severe dysplasias return to normal on their own. Alternatively, one could have the lesion frozen or burned or surgically cut out of the cervix.

However, if a pap smear shows actual cancer, the treatment is more complicated. It usually involves surgery, such as a hysterectomy (removal of the uterus), and sometimes involves radiation or chemotherapy. In any given year, over ten thousand women are diagnosed with cervical cancer, and almost four thousand women die from the disease.

How is HPV transmitted and how likely is my child to get HPV?

In the case of warts on the skin, the HPV is transmitted by direct contact with another person. There is often a minor cut or abrasion in the skin of the receiving person that facilitates transfer. This type of transmission is very common, and over 50 percent of children will develop warts at some time in their lives.

In the case of anogenital HPV, the virus is spread by direct sexual contact. Again, the virus is very common, and over 40 percent of sexually active teenage women have evidence of this infection. There is no data on the infection rate in men, but it is presumed to be as high as women because the virus is transmitted sexually.

What kind of HPV vaccines exist and when are they usually given?

There are two vaccines for HPV. The first to be approved was Gardasil, a vaccine aimed at HPV types 6, 11, 16, and 18. HPV types 16 and 18 cause over 70 percent of cervical cancer, while HPV types 6 and 11 are responsible for over 90 percent of genital warts. It is recommended for girls and women ages nine to twenty-six and is given in a series of three doses. The second dose is given two months after the first dose, and the final dose is given four months after the second dose.

The second HPV vaccine is called Cervarix. It has been approved in Europe and Australia, but approval in the United States is not expected until 2009. Cervarix only protects against HPV types 16 and 18, although cross protection against types 31 and 45 has been seen in one study. It is also a three-dose series but is given at zero months, one month, and six months. Cervarix is recommended for all girls and women ages ten to forty-five.

How effective is the HPV vaccine?

Both Gardasil and Cervarix are very effective in preventing cervical dysplasia and cervical cancer caused by HPV types 16 and 18. In studies involving thousands of women, the vaccines were over 95 percent effective in preventing cancer and serious dysplasia and over 80 percent effective in preventing milder dysplasia. Preventing mild dysplasia is useful because it reduces the need for additional testing and monitoring of lesions that often go away on their own.

Please remember that these vaccines do not protect against all types of HPV and therefore do not protect against all cases of cervical cancer. Thus they are not a substitute for regular pap smears.

How serious and how common are the side effects of the HPV vaccine?

The side effects of Gardasil are common (meaning more than 10 percent of recipients report them) but are mild and include pain, fever, swelling, and itching. These are all temporary and go away on their own. Although Cervarix has not yet been approved in the United States, information from international sources suggests that the side effects are also temporary and similar to those of Gardasil. They include pain, itching, swelling, and fever, plus a slightly increased risk for headaches, joint aches, nausea, vomiting, and diarrhea.

What are the medical reasons to not give the HPV vaccine?

The HPV vaccine should not be given to anyone who has had a severe allergic reaction to a previous dose of the vaccine or to any component in the vaccine, including yeast. In addition, people who are moderately or severely ill should be cautioned against receiving this vaccine until they recover from their illness.

Pregnant women should not receive this vaccine, not because it has been shown to be unsafe but because it is still being studied. There is no theoretical risk that an inactivated vaccine is able to harm the mother or the fetus, so if the vaccine is inadvertently given to a pregnant woman, it is not a reason to terminate the pregnancy.

What is Dr. Jamie's overall recommendation for the HPV vaccine?

I am very much in favor of this vaccine. It protects against cancer and precancerous cells and has minimal side effects. HPV is common in the community, and it is likely that most sexually active women will be exposed at one time or another in their lives. I feel the risk-benefit ratio is in favor of giving the vaccine.

I do recognize that we are talking about small numbers. For example, in one study of almost seventeen thousand women, fifty-three women in the placebo group developed severe dysplasia or cancer as compared to no women in the Gardasil group. While that shows 100 percent protection, there were still only six cases of the disease per one thousand women. In other words, you need to vaccinate a thousand women to prevent six cases of severe dysplasia or cancer.

However, as a practicing physician, I regularly run into abnormal pap smears that require additional time and energy on the part of the woman and the medical community. These abnormalities lead to more intensive testing, such as colposcopy, and also more treatments such as freezing or burning the cervix. While the number of actual diagnoses of cervical cancer is quite rare, there are ten times that many abnormal pap smears that this vaccine would prevent.

Finally, I want to say that while I favor this vaccine, I am not in favor of making this vaccine mandatory for school attendance as has been recommended in several states. While I believe in vaccines in general and in this vaccine in particular, I do not feel they should be mandatory. Instead, I respect the right of individual adults and parents to make medical decisions for themselves and their children.

Chapter 19

THE PNEUMOCOCCAL VACCINE FOR OLDER CHILDREN AND ADULTS

The pneumococcal disease and vaccines have already been discussed on page 107 in chapter 6. Remember that there are two pneumococcal vaccines. The vaccine for younger children, which is known as PCV7 and goes by the name of Prevnar, is available for children under the age of five. The vaccine for older children and adults is known as PPV23 and goes by the name of Pneumovax. It is available for individuals over the age of twenty-four months.

The PCV7 vaccine might be given to children over the age of twelve months as a booster dose or as a catch-up dose. Either way, it is recommended for all children. The PPV23 vaccine is only recommended for children who are at high risk for developing pneumococcal disease, with a booster dose recommended three to five years later. High-risk children include children with sickle cell disease, children without a functioning spleen, and children with certain immune deficiencies. It also includes children with certain chronic diseases of the heart or lungs (congenital heart disease or asthma) or diabetes. Note that there is a three-year time period where the two vaccines overlap, and in some special high-risk circumstances, both vaccines might be recommended for a given child.

I strongly recommend the pneumococcal vaccines. The PCV7 vaccine receives my highest recommendation of all childhood vaccines. I also strongly recommend the PPV23 vaccine, although there are fewer circumstances where that vaccine is needed. When it is needed, however, it is very safe and effective.

Part IV
Vaccines throughout Life

These chapters focus on vaccines that are recommended for adults in certain circumstances. It also discusses vaccines recommended for travelers, both children and adults, and finishes with a review of other vaccines available in the United States. Remember, if you don't have any concerns about vaccines, I recommend all the vaccines listed. I feel that the benefits outweigh the risks, both for the individual and for society as a whole. However, if you have some specific concerns, you can use the following questions to help you evaluate the risks and benefits of a given vaccine.

- What is disease X and what kind of problems does it cause?
- How serious and how treatable is the disease X infection?
- How is disease X transmitted and how likely is an individual to get disease X?

- What kind of vaccine for disease X exists and when is it usually given?
- How effective is the disease X vaccine?
- How serious and how common are the side effects of the disease X vaccine?
- What are the medical reasons to not give the disease X vaccine?
- What is Dr. Jamie's overall recommendation for the disease X vaccine?

Chapter 20

THE SHINGLES VACCINE

What is shingles and what kind of problems does it cause?

Shingles, which is also known as herpes zoster, is a reactivation of the varicella, or chickenpox, virus. When a person is exposed to the varicella virus, either by vaccine or by the normal disease process, the virus does not leave the body completely but lies dormant for many years in certain cells in the nervous system. Later on, usually when the immune system has been weakened, the virus can be reactivated and travel down the nerves to the skin. Groups of blisters appear on the skin in very well-defined areas. Where the rash appears is dependent on which nerve cells contain the virus. It can occur anywhere on the body but most commonly appears on the trunk.

In general, the rash itself is not significant, unless it occurs in a particularly sensitive area, such as around the eye. The blisters themselves only last a few weeks, and secondary bacterial skin infections are uncommon. However, the pain associated with the rash can last for weeks to months and, in some cases, years. The pain is often described as debilitating and can severely affect a person's quality of life.

How serious and how treatable is the shingles infection?

The pain from shingles occurs more frequently and lasts longer in the elderly and in patients with weakened immune systems. Children and young adults rarely have significant pain and thus rarely need any treatment for shingles. However, if an individual who develops shingles is at high risk for severe or prolonged pain, there are a variety of potential treatments. These include specific anti-viral medications such as acyclovir, famciclovir, or valocyclovir, which work best if started in the first three days of the rash. The role of steroids such as prednisone is controversial, with some studies showing moderate benefits and other studies showing no benefits.

If the shingles is accompanied by significant pain, there are many ways to treat the pain, depending on whether it lasts for days, weeks, or months. These include over-the-counter pain medication, narcotics, certain antidepressants and antiseizure medications, nerve blocks, lidocaine patches, and a certain pain cream called capsaicin. Capsaicin is an over-the-counter remedy that works to deplete the pain-impulse transmitter substance P in the skin where the cream is applied. Unfortunately, even with all these methods, the pain following shingles sometimes cannot be relieved, and affected individuals may suffer for months.

What kind of vaccine for shingles exists and when is it usually given?

The vaccine for shingles is a live, attenuated vaccine called Zostavax. It is recommended for any adult age sixty years or older. It is a very expensive vaccine, running over $150 for a single dose, and most health insurance companies do not cover the cost of the vaccine.

How effective is the shingles vaccine?

The risk of developing shingles increases as a person gets older. Adults face approximately a 30 percent risk of developing shingles between the ages of sixty and ninety years. The vaccine is not perfect, but it does decrease that risk by half. Interestingly, the studies show more benefits for those aged sixty to sixty-nine, where the risk was decreased by almost two-thirds. The oldest adults, over age eighty, only had a 20 percent decrease in risk.

How serious and how common are the side effects of the shingles vaccine?

The vaccine is very safe with only mild side effects, such as redness or pain and swelling at the injection site in one-third of recipients. Very rarely, some recipients experience headaches. These effects are temporary, going away in just a few days.

What are the medical reasons to not give the shingles vaccine?

The shingles vaccine should not be given to anyone who has had a severe allergic reaction to a previous dose of the vaccine or to any component in the vaccine, including egg protein. In addition, people who are moderately or severely ill should be cautioned against receiving this vaccine until they recover from their illness.

Because the vaccine contains a live, attenuated virus, it is not recommended for any person with a deficiency of the immune system. This would include anyone who has HIV or certain kinds of cancer, is receiving chemotherapy or radiation therapy, or has been on medications that suppress the immune system, such as steroids, for more than two weeks. It is also not recommended for anyone who is pregnant or might be getting pregnant (although that is unlikely for a woman over the age of sixty).

What is Dr. Jamie's overall recommendation for the shingles vaccine?

I strongly recommend this vaccine. If you live long enough, you have an excellent chance of developing shingles, and shingles can be miserable. The vaccine is even useful if you have already had shingles because it is possible to have two or three episodes in your life. The vaccine is effective and has very few side effects. When you play with the numbers, you see that you would need to vaccinate only seven sixty-year-old adults to prevent one case of shingles over the next thirty years of their lives.

Chapter 21 OTHER ADULT VACCINES

Which other vaccines are recommended for adults?

The shingles vaccine is the only new vaccine that is routinely recommended for adults; the other vaccines recommended for adults have been discussed previously in parts II and III of this book. In brief, if an adult failed to receive a vaccine as a child, it may be appropriate to receive it as an adult. Vaccines in this category include the Tdap and Td, pneumococcal, hepatitis A and B, HPV, MMR, chickenpox, and flu vaccines.

When should an adult receive the Tdap or Td vaccines?

Adults should receive a tetanus booster, usually Td, every ten years for as long as they live. In addition, if they have a particularly dirty wound and their last tetanus booster was more than five years ago, they should receive a tetanus booster while the wound is being treated. The Tdap vaccine should be substituted for the Td vaccine once in an adolescent's or adult's life. Healthcare workers and parents of newborn children are encouraged to receive a Tdap vaccine as soon as possible, even if they recently had a tetanus booster. This vaccine will decrease the risk of spreading pertussis to patients or newborns.

Adults who have never received the original series of three tetanus-containing vaccines should receive a series of three vaccines, each spaced a month apart. This series would include one Tdap and two Td vaccines.

For more details on the Tdap and Td vaccines and the diseases they protect against, see chapter 8.

When should an adult receive the pneumococcal vaccine?

All adults should receive the pneumococcal vaccine one time after age sixty-five. In addition, adults with certain chronic illnesses should also receive the vaccine regardless of age. These illnesses include emphysema, chronic heart or liver disease, diabetes, certain immunosuppressive conditions, alcoholism, renal failure or the absence of a functioning spleen. Usually one dose is all that is required, but in certain circumstances, a booster dose of the vaccine is recommended five years after the first dose. For more details on the pneumococcal vaccine and the disease it protects against, see chapter 6.

When should an adult receive the hepatitis A or B vaccines?

Adults should receive one or both of these vaccines when they are at higher than average risk of contracting Hepatitis A or B or of suffering if they develop either disease. For hepatitis A, the major risks are travel to developing countries or chronic liver disease. For hepatitis B, risk factors include chronic liver or kidney disease, HIV, or regular contact with body fluids, as with healthcare workers. It is also possible to spread hepatitis B when sharing needles used with IV drugs. Hepatitis B can also be contracted if you are living with or in close contact with someone who is a hepatitis B carrier. This is why residents of certain long-term facilities should receive the vaccine. Hepatitis B can also be spread sexually, so anyone with multiple sexual partners or with a sexually transmitted disease should receive the hepatitis B vaccination.

The hepatitis A and B vaccines can be given separately or in a combined single-needle vaccine called Twinrix. The schedule for the hepatitis A vaccine is one dose and a booster dose six months later. The most common schedule for the hepatitis B vaccine is a dose at 0, 1, and 6 months. If someone needs both vaccines, they can receive Twinrix at zero, one, and six months. The extra dose of Hepatitis A is not considered significant.

For more details on the hepatitis A vaccine and the disease it protects against, see chapter 15. For more details on the hepatitis B vaccine and the disease it protects against, see chapter 11.

When should an adult receive the human papillomavirus (HPV) vaccine?

There are two HPV vaccines: Gardasil and Cervarix. Gardasil is recommended for girls and women ages nine to twenty-six and is given in a series of three injections at zero, two, and six months. Cervarix is expected to be approved for use in the United States in 2009. It is recommended for girls and women ages ten to forty-five and is given in a series of three vaccines at zero, one, and six months. For more details on the HPV vaccine and the disease it protects against, see chapter 18.

When should an adult receive the MMR vaccine?

Adults born before 1957 do not need the MMR vaccine. The explanation for this recommendation is that nearly every person born before 1957 contracted the actual diseases when they were young and are thus presumed immune to measles, mumps, and rubella.

Adults born during or after 1957 should receive at least one dose of the MMR vaccine if they did not receive it in the past. Certain adults should receive a booster dose, which needs to be given more than four weeks after the first dose. People who should receive a booster dose include college students, healthcare workers, international travelers, and people exposed during a measles or mumps outbreak.

It is very common for pregnant women to have their blood drawn to see if they are immune to rubella. If they are not immune, they are usually given an MMR vaccine after the birth of their baby. However, the position of many vaccine experts is that if the pregnant woman has clear documentation that two MMR vaccines were given in the past, then the result saying that she is not immune is probably wrong and she does not need a booster.

If a woman is planning to become pregnant in the future and is not sure if she received two MMR vaccines in the past, she can have her blood drawn to see if she has immunity to rubella. If she does not have the necessary antibodies, she could then receive one (if only a low level of antibodies is present) or two MMR vaccines before she becomes pregnant.

Remember that she should wait at least twenty-eight days after the last MMR vaccine before becoming pregnant in order to avoid the theoretical risk of transmission of a live virus to her fetus.

For more details on the MMR vaccine and the diseases it protects against, see chapter 13.

When should an adult receive the chickenpox vaccine?

Studies have shown that when adults have a clear memory, either personal or from a parent, of having had chickenpox, they are over 99 percent likely to be immune. Interestingly, though, if an adult does not have any memory of having had chickenpox, he or she still has a 70 percent chance of being immune. This suggests that many people have such mild cases of chickenpox that they go unnoticed.

With this information in mind, for those who do not have any recollection of having had chickenpox in the past, there are two options. They can have their blood drawn and only receive the vaccination if they are not immune. Or they can simply receive the vaccinations without any blood test. Adults should receive two doses at least four weeks apart.

For more details on the varicella vaccine and chickenpox, see chapter 14.

When should an adult receive the flu vaccine?

All adults over the age of fifty should receive the flu vaccine at the beginning of the flu season, which is October or November in the United States. In addition, adults with certain chronic illnesses should also receive the flu vaccine annually. These illnesses include chronic respiratory problems like asthma or emphysema, chronic heart, liver, or kidney disease, diabetes, and HIV and other immunosuppressive illnesses. Women who will be pregnant during the flu season, healthcare workers, and residents of nursing homes or other long-term care facilities are also recommended to receive the flu vaccine.

For more details on the flu vaccine and influenza, see chapter 10.

Chapter 22 TRAVEL VACCINES AND OTHER VACCINES

- What are some common vaccines that are needed for international travel?
- Is there a vaccine for malaria?
- What are the risks and benefits of the typhoid vaccine?
- What are the risks and benefits of the yellow fever vaccine?
- What are the risks and benefits of the rabies vaccine?
- What should someone do if exposed to a rabid animal?
- What are the risks and benefits of the Japanese encephalitis vaccine?
- What are the risks and benefits of the BCG, or tuberculosis, vaccine?
- What are the risks and benefits of the anthrax vaccine?
- What is the vaccinia vaccine?
- Are there any other vaccines available in the United States?

What are some common vaccines that are needed for international travel?

A very important issue for all international travelers is to make sure their basic vaccines are up to date. This includes a tetanus vaccine within the last ten years, two MMR vaccines, two chickenpox vaccines or a clear memory of the illness, and a series of at least three polio vaccines. Depending on which country the traveler is visiting and during which time of year, a polio booster or the flu vaccine may be necessary as well. The flu season is different in different countries.

Additional recommended vaccines for international travelers might include the hepatitis A vaccine, if traveling in developing countries, and the meningococcal vaccine for certain equatorial African countries. The meningococcal vaccine has also been required by the government of Saudi Arabia for pilgrims traveling to Mecca in order to prevent a recurrence of the meningitis epidemic that occurred in the 1980s. If the traveler is likely to be exposed to human blood products, then the hepatitis B vaccine is recommended. Certain travelers with exposure to animals, especially spelunkers with exposure to bats, should receive the rabies vaccine.

Other common vaccines for travelers include the typhoid vaccine and the yellow fever vaccine.

Uncommon vaccines for travelers would include the Japanese encephalitis vaccine and the tuberculosis or BCG vaccine. A complete list of recommendations for travel to various countries in the world can be found in the Traveler's Health section of the CDC's website, at www.cdc.gov.

Is there a vaccine for malaria?

Unfortunately, there is not a vaccine for malaria. However, physicians can prescribe antimalarial medication if appropriate for the country to which you are traveling. There are different medications for different parts of the world, so you need to search the malaria section of www.cdc.gov for more information.

What are the risks and benefits of the typhoid vaccine?

Salmonella typhi is the bacterium that causes typhoid fever, an illness characterized by fever, fatigue, malaise, a lack of appetite, and often diarrhea. The bacteria are spread by direct contact with infected food or with an infected person's stool. There are currently several excellent antibiotics for treating the more severe cases of typhoid fever. In the past, the fatality rate was around 30 percent. Antibiotic treatment has lowered that to around 1 percent. However, given that there are between twenty and thirty million cases of typhoid fever a year, the illness still kills tens of thousands of people annually.

There are two typhoid vaccines. The injectable vaccine is a killed polysaccharide vaccine that can be given to anyone over the age of two. Each injection lasts for two years. The oral vaccine is a live, attenuated-virus vaccine and can be given to anyone over the age of six. It is given in a series of four pills every other day for a week. This series lasts for five years. The side effects for both vaccines are uncommon and minimal when they do occur. Most adults prefer taking the oral vaccine, as it lasts longer and doesn't involve a needle.

Neither vaccine should be given to anyone who has had a severe allergic reaction to a previous dose of the vaccine or to any component in the vaccine. Because the oral vaccine contains a live, attenuated virus, it is not recommended for any person with a deficiency of the immune system. This would include anyone who has HIV or certain kinds of cancer, is receiving chemotherapy or radiation therapy, or has been on medications that suppress the immune system, such as steroids, for more than two weeks. If a pregnant woman is a candidate for a typhoid vaccine, the injectable killed-virus vaccine is preferred over the live, attenuated, oral vaccine because of the theoretical risk that the attenuated virus could affect the fetus.

If there is no medical reason to not give the vaccine, I follow the CDC recommendations. If the CDC recommends this vaccine for a given country, then I also recommend this vaccine for a traveler to that country.

What are the risks and benefits of the yellow fever vaccine?

Yellow fever is caused by an arbovirus in the tropical regions of Africa and South America and is spread by mosquitoes. The illness starts out with a mild fever accompanied by a headache, malaise, nausea, and vomiting, and then resolves temporarily. It returns with more severe symptoms including a high fever, vomiting blood plus blood in the stool, jaundice, and heart and kidney damage. Over 50 percent of the cases are fatal.

The vaccine is recommended for all individuals over nine months of age who are traveling to or living in areas that have yellow fever. In addition, certain countries require proof of vaccination if you are arriving from a different country that has yellow fever, even if you only visited that country in transit. The fear is that you will pick up the virus and bring it to the uninfected country.

The yellow fever vaccine is a live, attenuated vaccine. Side effects to the vaccine occur in 25 percent of recipients, but most are temporary and mild. Unfortunately, about one in one hundred thousand recipients develop encephalitis related to the weakened virus in the vaccine. This encephalitis is more common in infants, which is why the vaccine is only recommended for children over nine months of age. In addition, about one in two hundred thousand recipients develop the actual yellow fever illness from the vaccine. As already described, the illness can be severe and fatal. Thus, while the disease is clearly dangerous, the vaccine has rare severe reactions as well.

The vaccine should not be given to anyone who has had a severe allergic reaction to a previous dose of the vaccine or to any component in the vaccine. Because the oral vaccine contains a live, attenuated virus, it is not recommended for any person with a deficiency of the immune system. This would include anyone who has HIV or certain kinds of cancer, is receiving chemotherapy or radiation therapy, or has been on medications that suppress the immune system, such as steroids, for more than two weeks. The vaccine should be given to a pregnant woman only if travel to a high-risk country is unavoidable and the risk of exposure is high.

If there is no medical reason to not give the vaccine, I follow the CDC recommendations. If the CDC recommends this vaccine for a given country, then I also recommend this vaccine for a traveler to that country. The yellow fever vaccine can only be given in certain travel clinics around the country. To find the closest yellow fever clinic near you, contact your local health department or go to http://www2.ncid.cdc.gov/travel/yellowfever/.

What are the risks and benefits of the rabies vaccine?

Rabies is a viral infection that occurs in animals, most commonly in bats but also in dogs, raccoons, skunks, foxes, and other wild animals. The virus is present in the saliva of infected animals and is transmitted to other animals or humans by bites or by contact between the infected saliva and broken skin or mucus membranes. By the time an infected human begins to have symptoms, there is no effective treatment, and the disease is almost uniformly fatal.

There are two killed-virus vaccines currently available in the United States for rabies. As of the fall of

2008, there is a manufacturing problem with one of the vaccines, with resultant shortages. The vaccine is recommended for travelers or animal healthcare workers who regularly come in contact with wild animals. Although dogs and cats are routinely vaccinated in the United States against rabies, people are not, mainly because the risk to the average person is so low.

The side effects of the current rabies vaccines are less common and less severe than with past rabies vaccines. Pain, swelling, and itching at the injection site are reported by up to 25 percent of recipients, while 10–20 percent report more general symptoms such as headaches, nausea, abdominal pain, and dizziness. With one of the vaccines, about 6 percent of recipients receiving a series of booster doses (for example, veterinarians) suffer a non-life-threatening allergic reaction with hives, swelling, and joint pains, plus fever, malaise, nausea, and vomiting.

In general, this vaccine should not be given to anyone who has had a severe allergic reaction to a previous dose of the vaccine or to any component in the vaccine. However, if a person has been exposed to a rabid animal, there is no medical reason to not give the rabies vaccine. Given the fatal nature of the disease, if the vaccine is required, it is given, and any allergic reaction will be managed as best as possible. The vaccine is safe to give to pregnant women and nursing mothers.

I recommend this vaccine to international travelers who might come in contact with wild animals. That might include researchers who are tagging and releasing wild animals but would not include people on a routine African safari. In the United States, I recommend this vaccine to veterinarians, animal-care workers, and others at high risk of exposure.

What should someone do if exposed to a rabid animal?

If a person is exposed to a potentially rabid animal, he or she should receive both the rabies vaccine and rabies immune globulin. The vaccine will help produce antibodies in the long run but take about two weeks to start working. The rabies immune globulin is an injection of antibodies filtered from the blood of other people who have had the vaccine. These antibodies can start attacking the virus in the blood immediately.

There are complicated rules as to who should get the vaccine and immune globulin based on what species of animal was encountered, what type of exposure occurred, and whether the animal was captured or not. The reason for capturing the animal, dead or alive, is so that it can be tested for rabies. If the animal does not have the disease, then the human contact does not need treatment.

One of the rules for giving the vaccine and immune globulin is based on a case report of human rabies that had been transmitted from a bat without a known scratch or break in the skin. In this case, a woman woke up to find a bat in her bedroom, which she let fly out the window. Since she did not recall any contact with the bat and it was felt that she would have woken up if the bat had touched her, she was not treated. Unfortunately, she developed rabies, presumably from an unknown contact with the bat.

For this reason, if a sleeping person wakes up to find a bat flying around in the room, they are advised to capture the bat, if possible, and to contact the health department for guidance. If the bat is not captured, the general rule is to treat the situation as if the bat had made contact with the sleeping person and to give the exposed person the vaccine and the immune globulin.

The vaccine is given in a series of five doses over twenty-eight days. If rabies immune globulin is necessary, it is only given once, when the person presents to medical attention. In general, the health department and emergency room are the most common sources of the vaccine and immune globulin, although some travel clinics may also have supplies.

What are the risks and benefits of the Japanese encephalitis vaccine?

Japanese encephalitis is a mosquito-transmitted arbovirus that is present in most countries in Asia. The disease is serious, with about one-third of those infected dying and about one-third of survivors having significant nervous-system problems remaining after recovery.

An inactivated vaccine is available for travelers who will be staying for extended periods (defined as greater than thirty days) in high-risk countries. Because there is a higher than normal risk of allergic reactions, although still low at only 0.6 percent of recipients, the vaccine is not recommended for travelers who are only spending a short amount of time in the high-risk areas. The vaccine is available for everyone over the age of one year and is given in a series of three injectable doses over thirty days.

This is a rarely used vaccine, and I have personally never needed to recommend this vaccine to anyone. However, given the serious nature of the illness, long-term travelers to certain parts of Asia should consider receiving the vaccine. I suggest that interested travelers review the information in the Traveler's Health section of www.cdc.gov.

What are the risks and benefits of the BCG, or tuberculosis, vaccine?

Tuberculosis is a disease caused by a mycobacterium that usually infects the lungs. It can be present in a latent form, where it is not actively harming the body, or in an active form, where the infection is spreading throughout the body. The active form of tuberculosis is contagious to others, but the latent form is not. The latent form of tuberculosis is usually treated with antibiotics in order to decrease the risk of it turning into the active form later in life. The active form of tuberculosis is much more dangerous and more difficult to treat with antibiotics.

The BCG (bacille Calmette-Guérin) vaccine is a live, attenuated vaccine for tuberculosis. It was named after two French scientists, Calmette and Guérin, who developed the vaccine, and is routinely used in countries with a high incidence of tuberculosis. Because of the extremely low incidence of tuberculosis in the United States, the BCG vaccine is not currently recommended in this country, except in very rare circumstances. Specifically, the

BCG vaccine is only recommended for children who are continually exposed to adults who have been ineffectively treated for tuberculosis or who have a multidrug-resistant strain of the disease. Alternatively, the vaccine is recommended for healthcare workers who are regularly exposed to multidrug-resistant strains of tuberculosis.

The BCG vaccine is only moderately effective, with an estimated 50 percent protection against active tuberculosis of the lung and up to 80 percent protection against active tuberculosis of other areas of the body. While these protection rates are lower than other vaccines, the disease is so common and so serious in high-risk countries that even that much protection is deemed worthwhile enough to use the vaccine.

The side effects of the BCG vaccine include local skin abscesses and enlarged lymph nodes in 1 to 2 percent of recipients. There are very rare reports of bone infections (osteitis) as well. Because the BCG vaccine contains a live, attenuated virus, it is rarely possible to contract active tuberculosis from the vaccine. About two in every one million vaccine recipients die from active tuberculosis contracted from the vaccine.

Because the vaccine contains a live, attenuated virus, it is not recommended for any person with a deficiency of the immune system. This would include anyone who has HIV or certain kinds of cancer, is receiving chemotherapy or radiation therapy, or has been on medications that suppress the immune system, such as steroids, for more than two weeks. It is also not recommended for anyone who is pregnant or might be getting pregnant due to a theoretical risk to the fetus.

The BCG vaccine is usually only given after consultation with your local or state health department.

What are the risks and benefits of the anthrax vaccine?

Anthrax is caused by bacteria that are usually found in animals but can spread to humans as well. There are a number of different forms of human anthrax, including cutaneous anthrax, which involves the skin, and inhalational anthrax, which involves the lungs. The average fatality rate is over 20 percent if the anthrax is untreated. In some severe cases, the fatality rate is near 100 percent, even with appropriate antibiotics.

Anthrax was in the news in 2001, when letters with anthrax bacteria were mailed to several news media offices and to two United States senators. These attacks infected over twenty people, and five ultimately died of their infection.

The anthrax vaccine is primarily given to military personnel and researchers or lab workers who work directly with the bacteria. In certain circumstances, veterinarians who work overseas or people who work with imported animal furs or hides might also be vaccinated. The basic vaccine series is a set of five vaccines at zero and four weeks, then at six, twelve, and eighteen months. In addition, there is a recommended booster every year after the initial series to maintain the protection from the disease. Over 95 percent of recipients develop antibodies to anthrax bacteria after three doses.

The mild side effects of the anthrax vaccine include soreness, redness, and itching, as well as a lump at the location of the injection. Other recipients may experience fevers, chills, nausea, headaches, muscle aches, and general malaise. These mild side effects usually go away on their own.

A moderate side effect listed on the anthrax Vaccine Information Sheet is a large area of redness at the location of the injection in 5 percent of recipients. A severe allergic reaction to the vaccine occurs in fewer than one in every one hundred thousand recipients.

The anthrax vaccine should not be given to anyone who has had a severe allergic reaction to a previous dose of the vaccine or to any component in the vaccine. The vaccine should also not be given to anyone who has survived a past exposure to anthrax, such as cutaneous anthrax. The vaccine is not recommended for women who are pregnant but can be given if there is a high risk of exposure to anthrax. People who are moderately or severely ill should be cautioned against receiving this vaccine until they recover from their illness.

What is the vaccinia vaccine?

The vaccinia vaccine is made from a live, attenuated vaccinia virus that is related to the smallpox virus. It was used in the past as a single-dose vaccine to protect against smallpox. In the United States, most adults over the age of forty still bear the one-centimeter-round scar on their upper arm that was left after receiving this vaccine as a child, due to the unusual way the vaccine was administered.

However, because of the successful eradication of smallpox from the world, the vaccinia vaccine has not been routinely given in the United States since 1972. It is now only used by laboratory researchers working with the vaccinia virus. Since the terrorist attacks of 2001, the United States government has prepared a smallpox response plan, which includes manufacturing enough vaccinia vaccine to vaccinate every person in the United States.

Are there any other vaccines available in the United States?

No, the vaccines listed in parts II, III, and IV of this book are the only vaccines currently available and approved for use in the United States. The Lyme disease vaccine was available in the past but was removed from the market by the manufacturer in 2002 due to low demand.

There are also many other vaccines available in other countries that are not approved in the United States. For example, Germany has approved a combination vaccine that includes DTaP, HiB, hepatitis B, and polio in one needle. These vaccines might become available in the future if approved by the FDA.

Part V
Vaccine Controversies and Myths

Chapter 23

Vaccines and Autism

- What is autism?
- What is thimerosal and why is it used?
- Why was thimerosal removed from childhood vaccines?
- What more has been learned about thimerosal since 1999?
- Were there any other consequences of removing thimerosal from vaccines?
- What is the story about the link between MMR and autism?
- Who is Hannah Poling and why did the Vaccine Injury Compensation Program (VICP) award her compensation for vaccine-associated injuries?
- So do we finally have proof that vaccines can cause autism?
- How many children with autism have a similar disorder to Hannah Poling?
- What does Hannah's case imply with regard to vaccinations for children?

What is autism?

Autism is a developmental brain disorder that affects a child's ability to communicate, appropriately interact with others, and form relationships. Autism is sometimes referred to as mind-blindness, or the lack of awareness of another person's point of view. Individuals with autism lack empathy because they cannot understand another person's perspective of the world. Autism usually appears before three years of age and often leads to idiosyncratic behaviors, such as hand flapping, as well as social withdrawal.

What is thimerosal and why is it used?

One of the best-known vaccine controversies involves thimerosal. Thimerosal is a preservative that contains ethylmercury. It has been used since the 1930s as a way to prevent bacteria from growing in a vial of vaccine. Before thimerosal was used, medical providers might inadvertently introduce bacteria into a multidose vial, thus contaminating the remaining vaccine. When a later dose of vaccine was drawn up from the vial, it would contain bacteria that could infect, or possibly even kill, the next vaccine recipient.

Why was thimerosal removed from childhood vaccines?

In the late 1990s, most vaccines used thimerosal as a preservative. In addition, there were a number of new vaccines containing thimerosal that were added to the recommended vaccine schedule for children in the first year of life. More vaccines with thimerosal meant each child was receiving more ethylmercury in the first twelve months of life. In the end, the potential amount of ethylmercury in the recommended vaccines exceeded the EPA-recommended maximum dose of mercury for infants.

While there was no proof that the ethylmercury in thimerosal was toxic, there was clear evidence that a related chemical, methylmercury, was harmful. The most famous example of methylmercury poisoning occurred in Minamata Bay, Japan, where an industrial company dumped mercury into the bay for decades. The methylmercury became concentrated in fish and shellfish, and subsequently affected people who ate the toxic fish. The results were catastrophic, with hundreds of people suffering from nervous-system symptoms such as an abnormal gait, abnormal speech, comas, and even death. Methylmercury also concentrates in the fetal bloodstream and leads to congenital methylmercury poisoning. This leads to birth defects and cerebral palsy in affected children.

Given the known risk of methylmercury poisoning, in July 1999, the American Academy of Pediatrics (AAP) and the U.S. Public Health Service (USPHS) recommended removing ethylmercury from vaccines as well as deferring the birth dose of the hepatitis B vaccine until the thimerosal had been removed. Since 2001, all vaccines that can be given to young children are thimerosal-free. The only exception is one version of the flu vaccine for children that still contains a trace of thimerosal, but less than 1 percent of the previous dose. However, there are other thimerosal-free flu vaccines available for children. Some vaccines meant for older children and adults still use thimerosal as a preservative. The supposed rationale for the remaining thimerosal is that older children and adults weigh more and are thus better able to tolerate larger amounts of ethylmercury.

What more has been learned about thimerosal since 1999?

Fortunately, recent research into thimerosal has not found any links between neurological disorders and the doses of ethylmercury found in vaccines. One specific concern was that thimerosal exposure might increase the risk of developing autism. However, population studies did not show any change in the rate of autistic spectrum disorders after thimerosal was removed from vaccines in Denmark and Sweden in 1992.

Another study evaluated over a thousand children with a battery of forty-two neuropsychological tests. These tests were administered to the children seven to ten years after their thimerosal exposure. The results were surprising. Only a few tests showed some relation to ethylmercury, but the results were almost equally divided between positive and negative results. This means that while a very few (less than 3 percent) of the tests showed that thimerosal hindered a neuropsychological skill, the same number of tests showed that thimerosal improved a similar skill. In the end, the random nature of these results, plus the majority of normal results, suggested that the noted associations were most likely due to chance.

Another study investigated the elimination of ethylmercury and methylmercury from the bodies of infant monkeys. It found that ethylmercury is eliminated from the body three to ten times faster than methylmercury, suggesting that ethylmercury is much less toxic than methylmercury.

In conclusion, multiple studies have not shown any relation between thimerosal and autism or other neuropsychological disorders.

Were there any other consequences of removing thimerosal from vaccines?

There is an interesting discussion in the public health arena about whether the removal of thimerosal from vaccines was actually harmful to the nation's public health. Remember that when the AAP and USPHS recommended removing thimerosal from vaccines in 1999 and deferring certain vaccines, there was no concrete proof that there was any harm from ethyl-mercury exposure. However, it was a plausible concern given the known toxicity of a related chemical, meth-ylmercury. Public health officials at the time felt it was a prudent decision, pending additional research.

An unintended consequence of the decision, though, was to diminish public trust in the vaccine supply. Both anecdotally in my own practice and statistically across the nation, many more parents became hesitant to vaccinate, even after the thime-rosal was gone. They regularly asked me about other ingredients in vaccines and worried about other unknown risks from formaldehyde or animal-tissue protein.

Over the past few decades, a lack of public trust in vaccinations has occasionally led to lower immunization rates in various countries. When these decreased rates occurred in Japan and Great Britain, small epidemics occurred of diseases that had been under control in the past. Statistically, if enough cases occur, then some bad outcomes will also occur. Indeed, with a mounting number of cases, some developed countries started reporting deaths from pertussis and measles.

This doesn't seem to have occurred in the United States in the last eight years, but it is a concern. In order to recommend the prudent course of action (avoiding mercury in vaccines), public health officials may have contributed to lower vaccine rates and increased the risk of contracting the disease. In short, they may have traded an unknown risk that appears to have been proven harmless for a known risk of increased disease.

Of course all this is in hindsight, and we now have reasonable evidence that the thimerosal in vaccines was not harmful. If ethylmercury had been shown to be harmful, the decision would have been applauded as brilliant and farsighted. But it does raise the question of what level of proof is necessary to act. Do you have to actually show that something is harmful? Or do you simply need a plausible theory?

When the CDC recommended against using the rotavirus vaccine in the late 1990s, it based its decision on hard evidence. There was clear proof of the increase in intussusceptions in the months following the administration of the vaccine. Should the U.S. Public Health Service have waited for similar clear proof in the case of thimerosal? But what about all the children who would be receiving the potential "toxin" while the research was being done? Can you justify harming some children while waiting for an answer? I have no clear answers to these questions.

What is the story about the link between MMR and autism?

In 1998, Dr. Andrew Wakefield and twelve other authors published a startling study that suggested a link between the MMR vaccine, inflammatory bowel disease, and autism. They found the measles virus from a vaccine (not the wild measles virus found in the community) in the bowels of twelve children with both inflammatory bowel disease and autism. They postulated that the virus somehow triggered the inflammation in the children's bowels, and that somehow led to autism.

The supposed link was widely publicized, and as a result, parents all over the world refused to vaccinate their children with the MMR vaccine. In some countries, such as Great Britain, the vaccine rate for MMR grew so low that small epidemics of measles occurred, with some deaths. Now, instead of a possible risk of autism, parents faced a real risk of disease and death from the resurgence of measles.

In my mind, this study should have been a call for more research to see if the association was real. With only twelve subjects in the study, it is hard to know if the results were just a fluke or a real finding. Many times in medicine, a small study suggests a finding that a larger study then proves is false. In general, one large study is better than several smaller studies. In this case, the authors used a small study to declare that the MMR vaccine was a cause of autism. Several authors of the original study have since retracted that interpretation, but many parents had already made the decision not to vaccinate.

Most other studies since 1998, including several very large population studies with hundreds or thousands of participants, have failed to find any link between the MMR vaccine and autism. The most recent study on the matter was published on September 4, 2008. It sought to exactly reproduce Dr. Wakefield's original study and compared twenty-five children with autism and bowel problems to thirteen children with bowel problems alone. The measles virus was found in only two children, one in each group, suggesting that it was not at all linked to autism.

In my opinion, the preponderance of the evidence suggests that there is no link between the MMR vaccine and autism. In addition, there is good evidence that autism has a genetic component. Twin studies show that if one identical twin has autism, the other twin has around a 90 percent risk of also having autism. However, fraternal twins have only a 10 percent risk of both having autism. This clearly supports a genetic basis for autism, as opposed to one caused by vaccines. I regularly reassure my patients that there is no increased risk of autism with the MMR or any other vaccine. Despite my reassurances, many parents still request delaying the vaccine and/or splitting the vaccine into its separate components.

Who is Hannah Poling and why did the Vaccine Injury Compensation Program (VICP) award her compensation for vaccine-associated injuries?

Hannah Poling is a young girl who developed an autism-like syndrome after receiving a series of vaccines in her second year of life. Subsequently, the Vaccine Injury Compensation Program (see chapter 4) reviewed her case and felt that there was a logical connection between the administration of the vaccines and the onset of her autism-like syndrome. Many people have used her story as an example of how vaccines can cause autism. In fact, however, it was actually the side effects of the vaccines that triggered her rare underlying cellular disorder, which then blossomed into a syndrome that resembles autism. So let's look at her story in more detail.

When Hannah Poling was nineteen months old, she received five vaccines in order to catch up on the recommended vaccine schedule. Those vaccines included DTaP, HiB, MMR, chickenpox, and IPV (inactivated polio). Two days later she had a fever with persistent crying that continued for several days. About ten days after the vaccinations she developed a rash consistent with chickenpox, presumably from the vaccine. Over the next several months, Hannah regressed developmentally and developed several symptoms of mild autism spectrum disorder.

After months of extensive and expensive testing, Hannah was ultimately diagnosed with encephalopathy due to a rare mitochondrial disease. The interesting fact about Hannah's situation is that children with this mitochondrial disorder usually develop normally until they are faced with a significant stress to their system. The stress may be a severe illness, a high fever, or significant dehydration. When the stress occurs, the mitochondria no longer function properly. Mitochondria are the energy plants of cells. When the energy runs low due to poorly functioning mitochondria, the cells are damaged, leading to complications like Hannah's encephalopathy. It was her encephalopathy that led to her autism spectrum disorder.

In short, children with Hannah's mitochondrial disease are susceptible to developing encephalopathy and developmental delays whenever their body faces a significant-enough stress. In Hannah's case, the stress appears to have been the vaccines, which led to the fever and the case of vaccine-associated chickenpox.

So do we finally have proof that vaccines can cause autism?

We need to be clear: the vaccines did not cause Hannah's autistic features. They merely caused the stress on her body, which triggered the mitochondrial disorder and the developmental regression. However, because the law allows for compensation whenever a vaccine is related to an adverse outcome, Hannah's family received compensation for her injuries. Had she not been vaccinated, she likely still would have developed autistic features from a different stressful event, such as a fever from a viral illness.

How many children with autism have a similar disorder to Hannah Poling?

That is difficult to tell. One study in Portugal showed that five out of sixty-nine (or 7.2 percent) of the autistic children who were studied suffered from a mitochondrial disorder similar to Hannah's. It is unclear if that percentage will be accurate across different countries and different populations of autistic children. It does suggest, however, that the majority of autistic children are not affected by this type of mitochondrial disorder. However, there may be other metabolic disorders that have not yet been discovered that contribute to autism.

It is also important to note that Hannah was able to receive extensive and very expensive testing, including a mitochondrial DNA analysis that showed the exact mutation that caused her problems. Most families are not able to arrange for such testing. For those who are interested, Hannah's father, Dr. Jon Poling, is a neurologist and published a scientific paper on Hannah and other children with autism. (See Resources.)

What does Hannah's case imply with regard to vaccinations for children?

Surprisingly, even though Hannah's symptoms started after her vaccinations at nineteen months, that does not imply she should not have received the vaccinations. Remember that her symptoms could have been triggered by any stressor, including a fever from a vaccine-preventable illness. The goal for children with Hannah's disease is to prevent unnecessary stress on their systems.

The question, therefore, is whether a child is more likely to develop stress from a side effect of the vaccine or from catching the illness itself. The answer depends on the illness. In the case of polio, the disease is so rare that the side effects of the vaccine are probably more common than becoming ill from the wild poliovirus. However, for other illnesses that are more common, such as chickenpox or pertussis (whooping cough), the trade-off might be different. In general, though, the recommendation is that for almost all children, the benefits of preventing a serious disease outweigh the risks of side effects from any given vaccine.

Chapter 24

OTHER VACCINE QUESTIONS AND CONCERNS

- Are there potentially harmful ingredients in vaccines?
- Is the aluminum in some vaccines a concern?
- Should I choose my vaccine schedule based on aluminum?
- Why is it true that the majority of people who develop a disease during an epidemic have already been vaccinated?
- What are "hot lots" of vaccines?
- What are the long-term side effects of vaccines?
- Does the flu vaccine cause the flu?

Are there potentially harmful ingredients in vaccines?

Vaccines contain a number of preservatives or additives. Most of them are in such minuscule amounts as to be considered harmless. For example, the product insert of the injectable polio vaccine states that formaldehyde comprises a maximum of 0.02 percent per 0.5ml dose. If you do the math, that works out to four ten-thousandths of a milliliter, which is a tiny amount indeed. The vaccine insert also describes how antibiotics are used in the manufacturing, but are processed out and remain at the level of nanograms. Just for perspective, there are one billion nanograms in a gram and there are thirty grams in an ounce.

Other ingredients in vaccines that worry some parents are the animal or human tissues used in the production process. Many vaccines are grown on animal cells, such as chicken eggs or monkey kidney cells. Between 1955 and 1963, some manufacturing lots of the polio vaccine were contaminated with a monkey virus: the simian virus 40, or SV40. SV40 has recently been found in several human cancers, including lymphoma. It is *not* clear if this virus is the causative agent of the cancer or is merely an innocent bystander. It *is* clear that while some of the people with SV40 in their cancer received the polio vaccine in question, many people with SV40 in their cancer did not receive that vaccine. So if SV40 causes cancer, there must be a way of getting the virus other than the contaminated polio virus of the 1950s and 1960s.

Unfortunately, we don't know if the SV40 contamination was significant. We do know that it is an example of the possibility of unknown side effects from vaccines. Although the current cell lines used for vaccines are screened for known infectious processes, some parents worry about infections that have not yet been discovered.

My response to this concern is that so far there is no evidence that this is a problem and that the manufacturers are doing the best they can to limit infectious organisms. While this is not conclusive by any means, it is most likely a small risk compared to the known benefits of the vaccine.

Is the aluminum in some vaccines a concern?

Aluminum is an ingredient that is present in vaccines in relatively high concentrations. Dr. Robert Sears has written extensively about his concerns regarding the amount of aluminum in vaccines, and I credit him for drawing many people's attention to this matter.

Aluminum is used as an adjuvant in several vaccines, which means that it is present in the vaccines to make the vaccine more effective. The aluminum also seems to make the vaccines more reactive, meaning it causes more side effects. For example, one HPV vaccine study compared a saline placebo with an aluminum-containing placebo with the Gardasil vaccine. (A placebo is an inert material that is designed as a control to study the effectiveness of the vaccine.) The results showed that the reactions of pain, swelling, and redness in the aluminum-containing placebo were significantly higher than the saline placebo and almost as high as the reactions from the Gardasil vaccine itself. This suggests that much of the reaction for this particular vaccine comes from the aluminum component.

It is clear that aluminum can accumulate and become toxic in certain populations with poorly working kidneys, such as premature babies and patients in renal failure. The FDA has limited the amount of aluminum present in certain IV solutions to avoid any risk of reaching a toxic level and suggests that the safe maximum dose in premature babies is 25 micrograms per day.

However, the FDA has not limited the amount of aluminum in vaccines. While not all vaccines contain aluminum, some common vaccines do (see the table on page 276). The amount of aluminum in those vaccines ranges from 125 to 850 micrograms of aluminum per dose of vaccine. When you compare this to the recommended dose in premature babies—and you recognize that healthy babies are given multiple vaccines at once—you see the concern.

My perspective on this issue is that Dr. Sears has issued a wake-up call for more research. We know that premature babies with poorly functioning kidneys who receive certain IV fluids can become aluminum toxic. We don't know if that information can be extrapolated to other populations. What about healthy six-month-old babies with normal kidneys who receive aluminum by injection into the muscle? How much extra protection does the extra weight and better kidney function offer? And how quickly is the aluminum eliminated when introduced intravenously versus intramuscularly?

I don't know how this research is going to turn out. It might be like thimerosal, where a plausible theory of harm has been generally disproved after several subsequent studies. Or it might end up like DTP versus DTaP. DTP was a whole-cell pertussis vaccine used in the past that was very reactive, meaning it had a large number of side effects. In the 1990s, the medical community switched to DTaP, an acellular pertussis vaccine that provides equal protection with fewer side effects.

I am very comforted by the fact that aluminum is a natural part of every child's diet. One study suggests that by six months of age, breast-fed children ingest over 6,000 micrograms of aluminum, while formula-fed children ingest between 30,000 and 120,000 micrograms. In contrast, the maximum dose of aluminum from vaccines in the first six months is around 3,000 micrograms. For a critique of Dr. Robert Sears's book, please see Dr. Paul Offit's article in the Resources section of this book.

Should I choose my vaccine schedule based on aluminum?

If you are worried about aluminum in your child's vaccines, you can ask your doctor which brand of certain vaccines he or she carries. For example, the Infanrix brand of the DTaP vaccine contains 625 micrograms of aluminum, while the Daptacel brand only contains 330 and the Tripedia brand only contains 170. As for the HiB vaccines, the ActHiB brand contains no aluminum, while the PedVaxHiB contains 225 micrograms. For more details on the amount of aluminum in certain vaccines, please see the table on page 276.

Armed with this information, you might make certain decisions about the vaccine schedule. For example, you might decide against Pediarix, with 850 micrograms, and instead choose a hepatitis B vaccine with less aluminum. The drawback would be that you are using three needles instead of just one for the combination vaccine. In addition, Tripedia, the DTaP vaccine that contains the least aluminum, still has a trace (less than 0.3 micrograms) of thimerosal in it. If you wanted to use Daptacel instead, you would be trading off 0.3 micrograms of ethylmercury for an additional 160 micrograms of aluminum.

Another choice might be to avoid giving two aluminum-containing vaccines on the same day. This would force you to come back for extra visits to stay on schedule. It might be tedious, but minimizing the amount of aluminum your child receives in a day might be worth it for you.

My recommendation is that your child should receive all the vaccines using whatever schedule makes you feel most comfortable. While I prefer and recommend the simplicity of the CDC schedule, I will work with the families in my practice to accommodate them in whatever way works best for them, with the final goal of achieving complete vaccination for their child.

Aluminum in Vaccines

Vaccine Type	Brand Name	Micrograms of Aluminum
DTaP	Daptacel	330
DTaP	Infanrix	625
DTaP	Tripedia	170
DTaP/Hepatitis B/Polio	Pediarix	850
DTaP/HiB/Polio	Pentacel	330
Hepatitis A	Havrix, Adult	500
Hepatitis A	Havrix, Pediatric	250
Hepatitis A	Vaqta, Adult	450
Hepatitis A	Vaqta, Pediatric	225
Hepatitis B	Engerix, Adult	500
Hepatitis B	Engerix, Pediatric	250
Hepatitis B	Recombivax, Adult	500
Hepatitis B	Recombivax, Pediatric	250
Hepatitis B/HiB	Comvax	225
HiB	PedVaxHib	225
HPV	Cervarix	500
HPV	Gardasil	225
Pneumococcal, pediatric	Prevnar	125
Tdap	Adacel	330
Tdap	Boostrix	390

The following vaccines have no aluminum listed in their ingredients: HiB (ActHIB brand), influenza (all brands), meningococcal (Menactra and Menomune brands), MMR, varicella/chickenpox and shingles (Attenuvax, MMR, Mumpsvax, Proquad, Varivax, Zostavax brands), adult pneumococcal (Pneumovax brand), polio (IPV brand), rotavirus (RotaRix and RotaTeq brands).

Why is it true that the majority of people who develop a disease during an epidemic have already been vaccinated?

While this statement is sometimes used in antivaccine literature to show that vaccines don't work, in truth it shows the benefits of vaccines.

Let's suppose that there are a thousand children in a school and that 90 percent of them have been vaccinated against chickenpox with a single dose of the vaccine five years ago. This means that nine hundred students have been vaccinated, and one hundred have not been vaccinated. We know about 15 percent of vaccine recipients do not have continuing protection after five years. This means that of the nine hundred vaccinated students, 15 percent, or 135 students, are no longer immune to chickenpox.

Now, let's expose all one thousand children to chickenpox. In general, 95 percent of children without immunity to chickenpox will develop the disease. For the one hundred unvaccinated students, ninety-five of them will develop chickenpox. For the nine hundred vaccinated students, 95 percent of the 135 students who no longer have protection, or 128 students, will develop the disease.

So the statement is true. The majority of people who develop a disease during an epidemic have already been vaccinated. In our chickenpox example, more vaccinated students (128) developed the disease than unvaccinated students (95). However, this is only because there were so many more vaccinated students to begin with. The percentages are what matter. Only 14 percent (128/900) of the vaccinated students developed chickenpox, compared to 95 percent of the unvaccinated students. The vaccine, even with a waning immunity over five years, significantly protected the vaccinated students from the disease. Moreover, the vaccinated students who did get chickenpox would generally have had a much milder case of the illness than the unvaccinated children.

What are "hot lots" of vaccines?

A "hot lot" is the name given by antivaccine groups to describe a given manufacturing lot of vaccine as particularly reactive, meaning it has had a larger number of side effects than other lots of the same medicine. It is believed by some that there have been hot lots recalled and destroyed because of such serious side effects.

It is true that some lots of various vaccines have been recalled in the past, but the problem was a concern that they were not effective enough. A review of the manufacturing process suggested that the quality control wasn't high enough and that the vaccines might not have provided adequate protection.

My research has found only one lot of vaccine that has been recalled due to possible side effects. In 1979, at the request of the FDA, Wyeth Laboratories voluntarily withdrew lot 64201 of the DTP vaccine because of reports of eight infants in Tennessee dying of SIDS within one week of receiving this vaccine, some within twenty-four hours of administration.

However, the report noted that when compared to the same months in the previous year, the number of SIDS cases in Tennessee was not significantly increased. This suggests that the finding of increased SIDS was merely coincidental. If lot 64201 had been associated with additional cases of SIDS, then there should have been more cases than in the previous year.

For those who believe in hot lots, the subsequent actions of Wyeth lends credence to the theory that corporations can't be trusted. As outlined in *A Shot in the Dark: Why the P in the DTP Vaccine May Be Hazardous to Your Child's Health* by Harris L. Coulter and Barbara Loe Fisher, internal memos showed that Wyeth decided to never again allow a cluster of vials from one lot to be sent to a single state or health department. Limiting the distribution of vials to no more than two thousand in one geographic region would make it less likely for any cluster of side effects to be easily noticed.

What are the long-term side effects of vaccines?

In general, vaccines are monitored for their *immediate* safety. So if a significant vaccine side effect occurs within days or a few weeks of administering the vaccine, then it will likely be noticed by the Vaccine Adverse Event Reporting System (VAERS).

The VAERS program accepts reports of potential vaccine side effects from both individuals and health-care professionals. The reports do not have to prove that the vaccine caused the problem. The researchers at VAERS simply want to know about any medical issues that occurred in close proximity to receiving vaccines. Information about VAERS can be found at http://vaers.hhs.gov/. If you would like to report a vaccine side effect, you can fill out the VAERS information online or print out a form and mail it to the organization.

Since 1990, the VAERS program has received well over a hundred thousand reports of medical events after vaccines. Over 85 percent of the reports are for mild and/or transient problems, such as fever, pain, or mild irritability. The remaining 15 percent include more serious experiences, such as being admitted to the hospital or requiring surgery.

The VAERS program was responsible for noting that the rotavirus vaccine approved in the late 1990s had a significant side effect. After a million doses of the vaccine had been given, a slight increase in the risk of intussusception was noted. Given that intussusception is a dangerous condition that often requires surgery and can occasionally lead to death, the CDC made the decision to withdraw the vaccine from the market. I view this decision as mark of confidence in the system: a problem was found quickly, and the vaccine was removed.

However, to my knowledge, there is not a good system for monitoring possible long-term side effects from vaccines. If a child develops juvenile diabetes five years after his last set of vaccines, most physicians are not likely to think of reporting that diagnosis to the VAERS system as a complication of vaccination. Even if they did, they would probably have a hard time proving this were so. However, some people have felt that certain autoimmune diseases, such as diabetes or multiple sclerosis, are linked to vaccines.

Possibly the best way to investigate these types of hypotheses is to use population studies. Several Scandinavian countries and a few large HMOs have the data to see if there is an association between a certain vaccine and a certain disease years later. So far the studies have not supported any theory of harm. I have to admit, though, that the research in this area is limited.

Does the flu vaccine cause the flu?

I regularly face this issue every flu season. After I recommend the flu vaccine to a patient, they look me in the eye and say, "Thanks but no thanks. I got the flu vaccine years ago and caught the flu two days later. I was in bed for days!" I trust my patients, and I'm sure they were sick and in bed after the flu shot. But no matter how hard I try, I can't convince them that their illness was a coincidence.

The simple truth is that the flu shot cannot cause the flu. The injectable flu vaccine is a killed-virus vaccine and is thus unable to give a recipient the flu. However the intranasal flu vaccine is an attenuated, live-virus vaccine and theoretically could give a recipient a mild case of the flu. The more common side effect, however, is merely nasal congestion.

Resources

Recommended Books

American Academy of Pediatrics. *Red Book: 2006 Report of the Committee on Infectious Diseases.* 27th ed. Elk Grove, IL: AAP, 2006.

Offit, Paul A., and Louis M. Bell. *Vaccines: What You Should Know.* 3rd ed. Hoboken, NJ: Wiley, 2003.

Sears, Robert W. *The Vaccine Book: Making the Right Decision for Your Child.* New York: Little, Brown and Company, 2007.

Books That Offer a Different Perspective on Vaccines

Cave, Stephanie. *What Your Doctor May Not Tell You about Children's Vaccinations.* With Deborah Mitchell. New York: Warner Books, 2001.

Coulter, Harris L., and Barbara Loe Fisher. *A Shot in the Dark: Why the P in the DPT Vaccine May Be Hazardous to Your Child's Health.* New York: Avery, 1991.

Romm, Aviva Jill. *Vaccinations: A Thoughtful Parent's Guide: How to Make Safe, Sensible Decisions about the Risks, Benefits, and Alternatives*. Rochester, VT: Healing Arts Press, 2001.

Recommended Websites

The Centers for Disease Control and Prevention (CDC):
  http://www.cdc.gov
Immunization Action Coalition:
  www.immunize.org
Vaccine Information Sheets:
  www.immunize.org/vis
Vaccine Adverse Event Reporting Service (VAERS):
  http://vaers.hhs.gov/
National Vaccine Injury Compensation Program (VICP):
  http://www.hrsa.gov/vaccinecompensation/default.htm
Vaccine exemptions:
  http://www.vaccinesafety.edu/
Travelers' health:
  http://wwwn.cdc.gov/travel/default.aspx
The most up-to-date vaccination schedules:
  http://www.cdc.gov/nip/recs/child-schedule.htm (for children) http://www.cdc.gov/vaccines/recs/schedules/adult-schedule.htm (for adults)

Vaccine information relevant to specific groups such
as college students or pregnant women:
http://www.cdc.gov/vaccines/spec-grps/default.
htm

Vaccine product inserts (the prescribing information
that comes with each vaccine from the manufacturer): Go to the website, choose the vaccine, and
choose the link to prescribing information.
https://www.merckvaccines.com/vaccineInfo_
frmst.html
http://www.vaccineshoppe.com/index.cfm?fa=
anon.piexpress
http://www.wyeth.com/vaccines

Dosing charts for acetaminophen and ibuprofen:
http://www.babycenter.com/0_acetaminophen-
dosage-chart_11886.bc
http://www.babyzone.com/baby_toddler_
preschooler_health/article/ibuprofen-dosage-chart
http://www.permanente.net/homepage/kaiser/
pdf/3533.pdf

Recommended Articles

An article showing that countries with lower vaccination rates against pertussis have between ten and
a hundred times more cases of pertussis compared
to countries with higher vaccination rates against

pertussis: E.J. Gangarosa et al., "Impact of Antivaccine Movements on Pertussis Control: The Untold Story," *The Lancet* 351, no. 9099 (1998): 356–61.

Dr. Andrew Wakefield's original study of twelve children with autism, who also were found to have lymph node hyperplasia in their bowels. Interestingly, this paper did not discuss the findings of measles virus in the lymph nodes; that came later. Six years after publication, ten of the thirteen authors retracted the paper's claims. A.J. Wakefield et al., "Ileal-Lymphoid-Nodular Hyperplasia, Nonspecific Colitis, and Pervasive Developmental Disorder in Children," *The Lancet* 351, no. 9103 (1998): 637–41.

This study duplicated Dr. Andrew Wakefield's original 1998 study, with very different conclusions: M. Hornig et al., "Lack of Association between Measles Virus Vaccine and Autism with Enteropathy: A Case-Control Study," *PLoS ONE* 3, no. 9 (2008), http://www.plosone.org/article/info%3Adoi%2F10.1371%2Fjournal.pone.0003140.

An article written by Hannah Poling's father about Hannah and how her mitochondrial disease manifested as autism. It also discusses how some children with autism have some differences in blood tests when compared to children without autism: Jon S. Poling et al., "Developmental Regression and Mitochondrial

Dysfunction in a Child with Autism," *Journal of Child Neurology* 21, no. 2 (2006): 170–72.

A comparison of the elimination of methylmercury and ethylmercury (thimerosal) from the bodies of infant monkeys showing that ethylmercury is eliminated much more quickly: Thomas M. Burbacher et al., "Comparison of Blood and Brain Mercury Levels in Infant Monkeys Exposed to Methylmercury or Vaccines Containing Thimerosal," *Environ Health Perspect.* 113, no. 8 (2005): 1015–21, doi: 10.1289/ehp.7712.

An article comparing neurological and psychological outcomes in over a thousand children exposed to different levels of thimerosal. There were few significant findings; some showed positive associations and some showed negative associations. The overall pattern was that the findings were related to chance: W.W. Thompson et al., "Early Thimerosal Exposure and Neuropsychological Outcomes at 7 to 10 Years," *N Engl J Med* 357, no. 13 (2007): 1281–92.

This article discusses a 1993 report by the Institute of Medicine that clearly links some adverse effects to vaccines: K.R. Stratton et al., "Adverse Events Associated with Childhood Vaccines Other than Pertussis and Rubella," *JAMA* 271, no. 20 (1994): 1602–5.

This article studied over two hundred thousand

children in thirty-one countries and found an association between the use of paracetamol (known as acetaminophen or Tylenol in the United States) and asthma and eczema: Richard Beasley et al., "Association between Paracetamol Use in Infancy and Childhood, and Risk of Asthma, Rhinoconjunctivitis, and Eczema in Children Aged 6–7 Years: Analysis from Phase Three of the ISAAC Programme," *The Lancet* 372, no. 9643 (2008): 1039–48.

This article contains Dr. Paul Offit's critique of Dr. Robert Sears's *The Vaccine Book*: Paul A. Offit, MD, and Charlotte A. Moser, BS, "The Problem With Dr Bob's Alternative Vaccine Schedule," *Pediatrics* 123, no. 1 (2009): e164–e169.

This article reviews the normal amount of aluminum an infant ingests in the first six months of life: Offit, P. A., and Jew, R. K. "Addressing parents' concerns: do vaccines contain harmful preservatives, adjuvants, additives, or residuals?" *Pediatrics* 112, no. 6 (2003): 1394–1401.

About the Author

Jamie Loehr, MD, FAAFP, has practiced as a family physician in Rochester and Ithaca, New York, for the past eighteen years. Although he provides a wide range of care, his first loves remain pediatrics and obstetrics. Jamie is married to his wonderful and supportive wife, Caitlin, and they are the parents of four young children.